Praise for *The Shopping Revolution*

"Barbara Kahn has captured what is at stake for those of us who serve customers: As retailers compete for their attention, their expectations will continue to increase, and meeting—not to mention exceeding—their expectations will become an ever-higher bar that many will fail to reach. Fortunately, in *The Shopping Revolution*, Kahn reveals what has enabled today's most successful retailers to thrive in the face of these challenges. An essential read for anyone who wants to keep pace with their customers and anyone who wants to understand the massive changes underway in retail."

—**Neil Blumenthal, co-CEO and co-founder, Warby Parker**

"In *The Shopping Revolution*, Barbara Kahn zeroes in on how a few formidable retailers have gained ascendance and offers advice to retailers on how to develop their own winning strategies. This is relevant for anyone who wants to compete with the retail superpowers of today and earn loyal customers. How retailers and brands engage with customers is undergoing a profound transformation and *The Shopping Revolution* provides a thoughtful framework on how to innovate in the new world of retail."

—**Oliver Chen, Managing Director, Cowen and Company**

"As Barbara Kahn powerfully argues, it is possible to compete in the era of rapidly changing shopping behavior. In *The Shopping Revolution*, Kahn dissects the strategies of leading retailers and offers powerful examples of how success can be achieved. A must-read for anyone who aspires to reach customers today—and tomorrow."

—**Marc Lore, CEO, Walmart eCommerce US**

"A masterful storyteller, Barbara Kahn expertly unpacks the strategies of today's seemingly unbeatable retailers. In the process, she shares their successes and failures and offers easy-to-implement takeaways. *The Shopping Revolution* is an indispensable guide for anyone who has a product to sell in the retail world."

—**Stuart Weitzman, Founder, Stuart Weitzman LLC**

"*The Shopping Revolution* is a comprehensive and fascinating read on the challenges facing retailers in these disruptive times. Sharing the stories of successful companies, Barbara Kahn offers a framework to structure strategic thinking and set the path for success. Highly recommended for anyone who wants to understand how to compete in retail—now and in the future."
—**Pierre-Yves Roussel, Member of the Executive Committee, LVMH (Louis Vuitton - Moët Hennessy)**

"*The Shopping Revolution* is ideal for those who want to gain insight into the dynamically changing retail industry. This great read covers the mechanics at play in a straightforward manner and will help readers understand the direction retailers must take to succeed."
—**Al Sambar, Managing Director, Kurt Salmon, part of Accenture Strategy**

"The disruptive forces bearing down on retailers leave little room for error. Yet those very forces have created a vibrant marketplace filled with opportunities. In her new book, *The Shopping Revolution*, Barbara E. Kahn reveals how leading retailers are generating strong growth and offers strategies for competing in an ever-shifting marketplace. I highly recommend *The Shopping Revolution* to anyone who wants to understand the changes in retail and learn how to outperform the competition."
—**Thomas Kingsbury, CEO, Burlington Stores**

BARBARA E. KAHN

THE
SHOPPING
REVOLUTION

How *Successful Retailers*
Win Customers in an Era
of Endless Disruption

Wharton
DIGITAL PRESS
Philadelphia

© 2018 by Barbara E. Kahn

Published by Wharton Digital Press
The Wharton School
University of Pennsylvania
3620 Locust Walk
2000 Steinberg Hall-Dietrich Hall
Philadelphia, PA 19104
Email: whartondigitalpress@wharton.upenn.edu
Website: http://wdp.wharton.upenn.edu/

Ebook ISBN: 978-1-61363-087-7
Paperback ISBN: 978-1-61363-086-0

I dedicate this book to my husband, Bob Meyer, who patiently and lovingly supported me through the book writing process, and to my children, Alyssa and Tim, who are always endless sources of inspiration.

Contents

Introduction: Disruption in the Retailing World

Call it an "apocalypse." Call it "disruption." Call it a "revolution." Whatever you call it, it is sweeping through retail, destroying old established brands and changing the very experience of shopping. In 2016 Sports Authority shut down 460 stores, Walmart closed 269, Aeropostale closed 154, Kmart/Sears closed 78, Ralph Lauren closed at least 50, and Macy's closed 100. The wave of destruction accelerated in 2017 with more than 8,000 store closings announced.

And it's not just chains reducing the number of outlets: Major retailers are disappearing from the landscape. Bankruptcy filings by US retailers nearly doubled in 2016, and in 2017, 20 more major retailers filed for bankruptcy protection, including such prominent players as Toys "R" Us, hhgregg, Gymboree, and RadioShack. Predictions for the near future suggest more retailers will follow suit.

It is clear that retail as we know it is changing, and with it, the very experience of shopping. Retailers face a radically transformed marketplace that poses some very significant challenges if they are going to be able to continue to compete—and if they are to avoid the vicious cycle of store closings and bankruptcy.

What is causing all of this disruption? What forces are responsible for the revolution in retail? I see seven major disruptive trends, beginning with the gorilla in the room, the game-changing dominance of Amazon.

7 Forces That Are Transforming Retail

There is no singular dynamic at play here. Rather, there are many different factors converging to change the face of global retail.

1. The Game-Changing Dominance of Amazon

The advent of Amazon has completely changed consumers' expectations about shopping. Beginning in 1997, Amazon introduced "1-Click" shopping, which eliminated the need for shoppers to reenter payment information every time they purchased. This started a long history of innovation where Amazon systematically removed the pain points in the shopping process. It introduced free shipping, unconventional return policies, dynamic pricing, and personalized recommendations and reviews.

Amazon also offered the "endless aisle," a very broad assortment with more than 1 million SKUs available online. It accomplished this by making it easier for small third-party sellers to sell online through Amazon Marketplace. In 2005 Amazon introduced Amazon Prime, the ultimate loyalty program, which now has tens of millions of members around the world. In 2006 the company launched Amazon Web Services (AWS) to allow small retailers to compete with bigger competitors by providing server capacity. Today the profitability that comes from AWS and fees from Amazon Marketplace allow Amazon to tighten margins even further in its retail business. Finally, Amazon continually innovates, from investments in robotics and drones to devices such Amazon Echo.

2. Omnichannel Shopping

There are also significant changes happening to the actual shopping process. People are buying more online; current estimates are that online shopping is about 30% of total retail. Mobile commerce has also grown, with some estimates suggesting an increase from 2% in 2012 to about 31% in 2016 in the United States.

With the ubiquity of mobile phones and their central role in the shopping experience, people expect to be connected to information continuously. They want instant gratification and on-demand fulfillment, and they expect high-quality shopping experiences. Everything is easier on the mobile. It is easier to get information, to click on a purchase, and to post a review. Mobile payments are also making it easier to shop in physical stores. From the retailer point of view, if consumers can be trained to use their mobile apps, the retailer can target consumers with promotions or information as they walk around the store.

But shopping is not really one channel or another; it is an omnichannel experience, which means that consumers expect seamless integration across all of these channels.

3. Massive Data Collection

With this seamless integration across all channels, it is now possible to record scads of customer data. Mining these data through artificial intelligence techniques allows retailers to personalize and customize shopping experiences.

Personalized offerings include deals that are offered individually at the right time, in the right place. Marketing in general is more tailored, and websites morph as a function of past behavior. Even in-store behavior can be individualized as consumers learn to use in-store apps to get price and product information.

Better use of data can help retailers to adapt to trends more quickly and provide better point-of-sale information. Better data also leads to more accurate forecasting, which can help retailers become leaner and more efficient and make logistics more effective.

To monetize the data in these ways requires both sophisticated data scientists and enough interaction with the customers to be able to collect enough data to draw conclusions. Some retailers like Amazon and grocers probably interact with consumers once or twice a week, while others, like department stores, may only be able to capture data from customer interactions two or three times a year. This suggests that the retailers who do not have high frequency of interaction may have to partner with other entities like Google or Facebook, or even other retailers or brands, in order to collect information.

4. New Technologies

In addition to the algorithms that are being developed from artificial intelligence and machine learning as a result of the collection of big data, there are important new advances in technology, both in the store and at home, which will change shopping experiences.

Retailers have high hopes for the advantages that will come through virtual reality and augmented reality. Already it is possible for customers to explore a complete virtual reality environment in order to determine whether they want to buy a particular product. For example, if one is considering buying a tent, that tent can be observed on the mountaintop in 3D; one can walk around it and get inside it.

Augmented reality is also being used by some progressive retailers. In the beauty category, customers can put virtual makeup on their real faces. In home design, customers can put a virtual couch in their real living rooms. Warby Parker uses a combination of facial recognition and augmented reality to allow consumers to try on their glasses; soon this will extend to eye exams.

Some stores in Beijing and Shanghai are also experimenting with contactless shopping, or high-tech fully automated stores that are unmanned and allow people to buy products without checkout lines. Amazon has stores that allow this type of shopping but it has not eliminated the sales associates. Walmart is experimenting with a contactless shopping store that will open in Long Island at the end of 2018.

5. Vertical Integration

Vertical integration is about integrating the retail value chain so the brand does the manufacturing, branding, and distribution. Products can go directly from the factory to the consumer or through the brand's own retail store or showroom, eliminating the need for the multibrand retailing channel and those corresponding margins. This typically allows for higher-quality products to be sold at lower prices.

Luxury brands are also going direct—not necessarily to lower prices, but to increase service, customization, and preservation of the brand narrative.

Many of the new "digitally native vertical brands" competing on high quality at lower cost feature price transparency as part of their customer value. Vertical integration has allowed for shorter delivery times, better return policies, and full access to information and inventory.

Vertical integration can also protect some retailers and brands from having to deal with Amazon's ruthless pricing strategies. The advantages of vertical integration are the potential for lower costs and higher control of quality and customer experience. There can also be better control of the supply chain, thus providing inventory management benefits. On the other hand, direct distribution can involve a great deal of startup capital and infrastructure, and it is often easier for small startups to scale by jumping aboard a well-established retailer like Amazon or the department stores.

6. Over-Storing of America

Even without all of these changes in technology and data collection, there was bound to be a shakeout in physical retailing because America is "over-stored." There is just too much supply.

Between 1970 and 2013 the number of malls in the United States grew more than twice as fast as the population. The United States has five times more shopping spaces per capita than the United Kingdom and 10 times more than Germany.

The industry has been building new stores faster than consumers can spend in them. There are several reasons for the missed forecasts. In some cases, developers were building more stores in areas where the population was decreasing, like in Cleveland. In other areas, like Phoenix and Atlanta, stores were built in anticipation of population increases that didn't occur because of the housing bubble. The Great Recession didn't help, as people started spending less. Stores are also in the wrong places: Demographics trends showed people moving back to the cities, but a lot of the stores were in suburban malls. Mall visits declined 50% between 2010 and 2013. And when anchor stores like Macy's fail, they take down the whole mall.

In response, smaller footprint stores are being built now, particularly in urban areas. Retailers are changing their format from selling to showroom to support online shopping. They are also developing distribution centers where customers can pick up online orders or make returns or exchanges. We are also seeing more pop-up stores, which can offer better economics because they do not need to be open 365 days a year, nor do they need to be permanently outfitted. Instead, they can be used strategically for short-term advantage for building brand awareness, promoting innovation, and supplementing high-demand seasonality.

Meanwhile, some of the stronger retailers and brands are opening big, beautiful flagship stores in global centers of commerce. These flagship stores are not necessarily designed to sell product but rather to build brand and provide loyalty-enhancing interactive experiences.

7. A New Generation of Customers: Generation Z

The media has been replete with discussion of the power of millennials. Accenture estimates their spending power will be somewhere around $1.4 trillion by 2020, representing 30% of all sales. But there is a new generation in town. Generation Z, or "Gen Z"—those born starting in the mid-1990s and just entering college now—will make up 40% of the consumer base by 2020; they currently influence family spending as well. One estimate puts their buying power at $44 billion.

One big difference between millennials and Gen Z'ers is that millennials experienced the Great Recession, while Gen Z grew up in flusher times. This makes them somewhat less price conscious. They are also more attuned to sustainability issues.

Gen Z'ers are not as brand loyal as past generations because they are used to seeing new digital brands spring up virtually overnight, and they are comfortable giving up their personal data—but they are sophisticated enough to demand that their data be protected. Like millennials, Gen Z consumers are digitally native and comfortable with online shopping. But these new shoppers are not shunning physical stores. What they do have, however, is different expectations for their store experiences. They expect and embrace technology in stores; they are comfortable with interactive shopping screens, self-checkout, virtual try-on, and other experiences. While they expect stores to offer fun experiential interactive shopping experiences, they also expect ultimate convenience as well. And those stores that don't deliver fall out of their favor.

Gen Z'ers do not want "things." They want experiences. Partly this is because they get currency from sharing photos on social media. They are more likely to rent or share products; they don't need to own things. As they embrace these trends, older Americans follow.

Gen Z'ers are also comfortable omnichannel shoppers and are quite used to using their phone in tandem with their in-store shopping. They value consumer reviews. They are sophisticated with price comparisons; they have more access to price data and use price calculators. But that doesn't mean they don't appreciate luxury. Like other generations there is great heterogeneity in price sensitivity.

They are also comfortable searching for information for themselves before they make purchases, so they are more demanding, and they expect more from in-store sales associates. Social media is just part of their everyday life. They share photographs of experiences and products with their networks.

How Can Retailers Compete in This Marketplace?

One of the keys to both Amazon's success now and Walmart's success in disrupting retail in the mid-nineties is a fierce understanding of what customers want. Winning retailers have to be completely customer-centric. This means they need to be mindful not only of what products customers want, but also of the importance of convenience—of removing the pain of shopping.

In addition, given how competitive the marketplace is today, it is not only important to fill customers' needs, but to do so in a way that is even better than the competition. This requires not only massive amounts of customer data, but also keeping track of competitive actions and anticipating future innovation and response. Finally, it is essential to keep pace with ever-changing technologies.

As scary as the Amazon threat appears to many, there are still a number of retailers who are doing quite well in this new world. That is the ultimate purpose of *The Shopping Revolution*—to explain how they are doing it. Not only do I identify and break down Amazon's remarkable strategy, I explain how other retailers' strategies are still generating strong profits and growth.

Why I Wrote This Book

As professor of marketing at The Wharton School of the University of Pennsylvania, I have had the unique opportunity to study the changing retail landscape for many years. Most recently, I directed the Jay H. Baker Retailing Center at The Wharton School, from January 2011 through July 2017.

Throughout those years I had extensive conversations with CEOs and C-suite executives of the largest retailers in the country, including Macy's, Saks, Lord & Taylor, Nordstrom, Ralph Lauren, Tory Burch, Costco, Walmart/Jet.com, Victoria's Secret, Barneys, LVMH, Estée Lauder, Stuart Weitzman, Sephora, Michael Kors, Coach, PVH, Alice and Olivia, Burlington, Perry Ellis, Vince, Ascena, Spirit, Walgreens/Duane Reade, Haddad Brands, Modell's, and Williams-Sonoma, among many others. I have also had the opportunity to work with some of the newer startups like Warby Parker, Bonobos, Birchbox, Harry's, Allbirds, Glossier, Story, Tommy John, Eataly, Rebecca Minkoff, and many others.

In addition to these conversations, I religiously read the retailing trade journals and newsletters, and, of course, conducted my own basic primary research in which I was trying to understand and predict consumer decision-making in retailing and health services contexts.

My deep immersion in retail research led me to understand what it takes for companies to compete now. I have distilled those insights into a strategic framework that explains both how successful companies are surviving and thriving in today's retail environment and where opportunities exist for retailers that need a more competitive strategy, as well as startups looking for a way in.

In chapter 1, I introduce the Kahn Retailing Success Matrix, which is built on two simple marketing principles:

1. Customers want to buy something they want (product benefits) from someone they trust (customer experience).
2. In order to win customers, retailers must offer products and experiences that are better than the competition's.

In the chapters that follow, I break down the strategies of dozens of winning companies using this matrix. In chapter 2, you'll read about how Amazon's laser focus on customer convenience has been a winning strategy. In chapter 3, I explore how Walmart and other retailers leverage low prices to be leaders. In chapter 4, the focus is on how vertically integrated brands are winning, from Warby Parker, Bonobos, and Casper to Trader Joe's and Zara. In chapter 5, you'll learn about the retail strategies for luxury, where low prices and accessibility are undesirable. Finally, in chapter 6, we'll look at how to compete on customer experience. Eataly, Story, the treasure hunt experiences offered by Costco or T.J.Maxx, or the exciting ever-changing beauty landscape in Sephora all demonstrate the lure of emotional and sensory engagement.

As Al Sambar, a retail expert at Kurt Salmon, says, "If you understand your customer enough to be the exclusive provider they trust to bring them a product or service they desire, then you have nothing to worry about from Amazon. But most brands should assume their consumers interact with Amazon 10 to 50 times more frequently than they do in their current distribution channels. Trust follows frequency. Amazon is winning frequency in a landslide. So even the best brands must be wary."

Competing in this ever-changing marketplace isn't easy, but it can be done if you're committed to starting the journey now.

Chapter 1

Gain a Competitive Edge: The Kahn Retailing Success Matrix

In This Chapter
- The Kahn Retailing Success Matrix
- Four Leadership Strategies That Offer Superior Value

H ow did Amazon become the retailer of choice for a large portion of the US population? How did Walmart beat out other grocers in the late 1990s to become the leader in food retailing? How did Warby Parker make a dent in the once-untouchable Luxottica's lucrative eyewear business? How did Sephora draw customers away from once-dominant department stores to become the go-to retailer for beauty products?

The answer is that each of these retailers raised customers' expectations in at least one key dimension of value: Walmart focused on low cost. Amazon looked to convenience. Warby Parker offered hip, branded eyewear to millennials. And Sephora strived to provide a superior in-store customer experience. Each, then, became the market leader to targeted segments of customers, and enjoyed enormous success.

But in today's competitive world of retailing, keeping a leadership position based on only one aspect of customer value—one area of excellence—is not sufficient. That's why each of these companies has also leveraged their inherent advantage in one dimension and offered excellence on a *second* dimension.

Today, Amazon not only offers convenience in shopping, but also guarantees very low prices. Walmart purchased Jet.com to augment its lowest-price platform and provide online convenience. Warby eliminated the middleman to offer glasses directly to the end user, and thus was able to provide significant cost savings. Sephora built a huge loyalty program that combined their in-store and online experiences to build a personalized, convenient experience for each of its customers.

These retailers offer individual examples of successful strategies. To generalize these successful approaches so that any retailer can map out their own strategic plan, I built a framework that is flexible enough to be used across different retailing verticals and different customer segments. In this chapter I break down this framework and explain the implications for implementing its strategic guidelines.

Mapping Successful Retail Strategies: The Kahn Retailing Success Matrix

Most classic frameworks of retail strategy are missing a critical dimension: the customer perspective. It is a significant and startling omission.

After all, when customers go shopping, they want to buy something they *value* (product benefits) from someone they *trust* (customer experience). Whether customers buy these products offline or online is a function of where they are, who they are with, and how much time they have.

A related insight that many retail strategies seemingly forget is that today, more than ever, customers have lots of choices and they gravitate to the retailers who offer them the best value on the dimensions they care about. In other words, retailers have to provide some kind of *superior competitive advantage* beyond what is being offered by the competition. This superior value can be delivered either by providing more pleasure and benefits for their customers or by removing pain and inconvenience from the retail experience.

Figure 1.1. The Kahn Retailing Success Matrix

These two ideas result in a simple 2 × 2 matrix that is surprisingly effective at categorizing the most successful retailing strategies today. The framework is very flexible and is relevant across different retailing verticals. Plotting strategy on this framework also provides a mechanism to measure progress at delivering this value relative to the customers' expectations and competitors' actions (see Figure 1.1).

The "Retail Proposition," the horizontal axis of this 2 × 2 matrix, represents the first principle: Customers want to buy something they want (product benefits) from someone they trust (customer experience). "Superior Competitive Advantage," the vertical axis, represents the second principle: In order to win customers, retailers must offer products and experiences that are better than the competition's.

This matrix spells out four basic strategies. The first two strategies, illustrated on the top row, differentiate themselves by offering more pleasure and more benefits; the second two strategies, illustrated on the bottom row, differentiate by eliminating pain points.

1. Lead on Brand: Offer Branded Product Superiority

Retailers in the Product Brand quadrant offer branded products that provide more differentiation, more value, more pleasure, and ultimately more *confidence* to a particular customer segment, as compared to other products on the market. Here I am specifically referring to the value that comes from *branded product*. It is the product's brand equity that brings the customer into the store.

There are several ways retailers can leverage the value offered through products that have strong brand equity. First, there are multibrand retailers who carry multiple lines of strong branded products that "pull" the customer into the store. Good examples include Nordstrom, Saks, Best Buy, or Kroger. The retailer's own brand name (e.g., Saks) may also be a draw, but here the differentiated focus is on the well-known and well-respected branded products. These retailers may also offer private-label or store brands, but these private-label brands typically differentiate by offering some kind of price advantage—rather than quality and superiority offered by the more powerful brands.

Other retailers in this quadrant will include high-quality brands that are sold directly to the end user. These are known as vertical brands and the product brand name is the same as the retailer's brand name. Examples include luxury brands like Louis Vuitton or Hermès, specialty retailers such as Lululemon or Zara, or the newer digitally native vertical brands such as Warby Parker or Glossier.

In all of these cases, these brands have developed deep emotional connections with consumers and a strong narrative; their customers frequently become brand advocates. In the luxury markets, these brands have heritage, exclusivity, and prestige. For the nonluxury brands, they have strong identity and values that resonate with their devotees. These brands offer a "point of view"—and a brand culture that consumers want to be associated with.

In addition to strongly branded products, retailers who excel in this strategy are typically very good merchants. Retailing analyst and journalist Walter Loeb describes merchandising as the "instinctual ability to choose the right items to round out merchandise presentations." He continues: "The best merchants intuitively know how to select products with care and make sure that their newest assortments are fashion-right, fresh, attractive and in sync with other merchandise their buyers had bought before."

Retailers in this quadrant also excel in design and style. The challenge is to be able to accurately predict the "next" trend. The product assortments have to be easy to process and aligned with the brand values; this usually involves curation (especially in physical stores) or the right filtering and categorization structure if the assortments are online, as well as catering to the "long tail." Finally, leaders in this quadrant may also compete on state-of-the art technology. All in all, the leaders here succeed in developing an innovative culture where new ideas are embraced and commercialized quickly.

2. Lead on Experiential: Offer Enhanced Customer Experience

Retailers in the Experiential quadrant offer a physical customer experience that provides more pleasure, more excitement, and more *fun* than other retailers can provide. Good examples are Eataly, Whole Foods, Story, Build-A-Bear, and Sephora. Here, the customer journey is more experiential, and is seen as a lifestyle choice, not a chore. This is a high-touch, social experience.

Even traditional retailers can add experiential components to routine shopping tasks. For example, Duane Reade has divided its stores into health, beauty, and food centers—each of which offers high-touch experiences such as clinical access, hair and nail services, and in-store food services. Costco makes the shopping experience fun by training customers to understand that they cannot ever know for sure which brands will be carried at any particular time. This promotes excitement and discovery in-store. T.J.Maxx and Burlington also promote this kind of treasure hunt experience, which encourages customers to come back to the store frequently to see what unexpected brands and styles may be available. Further, the customer journey does not have to stop at checkout.

For example, Blue Apron, Hello Fresh, and Plated have changed the food shopping experience: They do the shopping for the consumer, but their value-add here is actually helping the consumer prepare the food themselves. The food is premeasured and recipes are included, so here the customer experience is in the consumer's own home, not in the store. Retailers who offer subscription services, like Harry's, Stitch Fix, or Birchbox, also bring the customer experience into the home.

Other experiential retailers offer education. For example, Eataly and HEB offer cooking and wine classes as well as catering services. Sephora and Ulta allow customers to experiment and learn about their products with hands-on access. Showroom models, like those of Warby Parker and Bonobos, allow customers to touch and feel the product, interact with knowledgeable sales associates, and then purchase the products they want online.

Other retailers augment the customer experience in-store by becoming community centers and hosting events such as book readings, celebrity talks, and community get-togethers. Lifestyle brands often offer aerobic classes, rock climbing walls, and basketball courts. Pop-up stores within stores offer excitement, "newness," and innovation.

Experiential components can also be added by digitizing the shopping experience end to end so the physical store experience can build on information gleaned from online behaviors. For example, retailers can use in-store beacons, smart mirrors, or interactive display panels to connect consumers' in-store shopping patterns with their online behaviors—and then offer customized advice, suggestions, and promotions.

This type of total digitized experience presents a real opportunity for retailing in the future. Several studies have shown expectations in this domain are very low for most retailers, and according to a 2016 Kurt Salmon study, 60% of in-store digital experiences are perceived as average or below average by the customer. Another study by nChannel shows that 84% of consumers believe retailers are not doing enough to integrate online and offline experiences.

3. Lead on Low Price: Offer Operational Excellence, Lowest-Cost Efficiencies

Retailers in the Low Price quadrant provide reliable products or services at the lowest prices, and therefore offer customers the best *savings*. Retailers who can consistently offer the lowest prices have developed operating models that can efficiently manage inventory, keep overhead costs down, eliminate unnecessary intermediary steps, and reduce transaction costs at every step. Good examples include Walmart, Costco, T.J.Maxx, and Burlington.

Retailers that deliver operational excellence strategies, as defined originally by Michael Treacy and Fred Wiersema in *The Discipline of Market Leaders* (1995), are companies that look for creative ways to minimize overhead costs and to eliminate unnecessary transaction costs. They also offer reliability and efficiency, excellent customer service, and strong customer-focused policies for returns. These retailers build their entire business models around these goals.

The leaders in this category often identify a creative means for achieving cost advantages over and above the competition. For example, in pursuing a low-price strategy, Warby Parker founders and co-CEOs Neil Blumenthal and Dave Gilboa recognized that if they sold eyeglasses directly to the end users online (when 98% of the purchases were historically made in physical stores), they could reduce margins significantly.

In the 1960s, Sam Walton, who founded Walmart, recognized that the "high-low" pricing strategies that were being used by most grocers at the time resulted in uneven demand and high costs in managing inventory and distribution. To correct these inefficiencies, he implemented an "everyday low pricing" (EDLP) strategy that allowed Walmart to significantly reduce costs by reducing the costly peaks and valleys in demand. He supplemented these costs savings by revolutionizing the way retail companies manage their supply chain. Walmart practiced unprecedented coordination with their suppliers, sharing real-time sales data with the manufacturers who stocked their shelves.

4. *Lead on Frictionless: Offer Comprehensive Customer Understanding and Total Convenience*

Retailers in the Frictionless quadrant prioritize providing a frictionless customer experience that eliminates all pain points and offers the customer the *easiest* and most convenient way to shop. The key deliverable here is a simple, seamless integration of the shopping experience across all touchpoints. This requires the collection, capture, and analysis of all available customer data. Constantly analyzing the data allows for customization and personalization. The best example here is Amazon—first through its online platform, subsequently via its integration to physical store pickups, lockers, and its own stores, and eventually to the data collected in the connected home. Amazon also competes effectively in this quadrant by offering one place to shop for all of one's needs. Amazon has been called the "everything store." This ability to buy whatever you want whenever you want makes shopping more convenient and easy. This also allows Amazon to have more interactions with the consumers, which provide more data.

In order to succeed here, retailers must identify the current pain points in the shopping experience. For example, based on a survey of more than 2,000 consumers conducted in February 2017 by the Adyen payment platform, the most common consumer pain point in *physical* stores—one mentioned by more than 75% of respondents—is waiting in line; the second most common complaint focused on pushy salespeople, with the third being pressure to make a purchase in the store.

Other surveys have delivered similar results, with more respondents than ever before indicating they would rather interact with their mobile phone when shopping in-store than actually talk to a salesperson. However, these trends should not be read as an indication that there is no value to the physical location; in contrast to the complaints, 60% of the respondents indicated that they enjoyed the ability to touch and try on products in stores, as well as the instant gratification of walking away with a purchase.

Taken together, these data suggest that a key deliverable for retailers operating in this quadrant has to be a painless, seamless integration of the shopping experience across all consumer touchpoints. The challenge here is what Kurt Salmon consultants called the "digital experience paradox." In this world of the Internet of Things, the digital touchpoints are increasing—but notably these touchpoints are controlled by the consumer not the retailer. So, retailers must leverage the data, gain consumers' total trust, and proactively meet their needs in order to keep them loyal.

Loyalty metrics such as customer acquisition and retention costs, lifetime value of the customer, and churn rates help retailers identify their most profitable customers and make sure their needs are being met. Retailers who are succeeding in this quadrant are constantly increasing the number of touchpoints they have with their customers and using machine learning, artificial intelligence chat bots, and other strategies to systematize the customer experience and proactively anticipate customers' future needs and desires.

The customer benefits from each of these four quadrant strategies are shown in Figure 1.2.

Figure 1.2. The Kahn Retailing Success Matrix: Successful Strategies

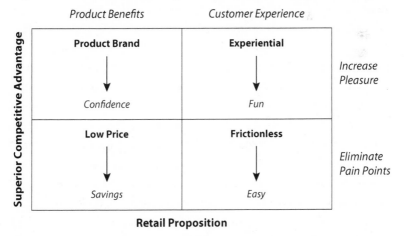

Plotting Retailers' Competitive Positions on the Kahn Retailing Success Matrix

The Kahn Retailing Success Matrix provides a way to categorize different winning strategies, but it doesn't on its own provide strategic guidance. To add that dimension, it is useful to think of the center point of the grid as the origin or (0,0) point of each of the four separate axes. On each of these axes, we can plot customers' perceptions for any retailer at delivering value given that specific strategy. The further out (i.e., toward the four corners) retailers are on each of the axes, the better their performance on that dimension; the closer they are to the (0,0) point, the less effective the retailer is at delivering the value. For example, if a retailer's performance on the experiential store experience axis is plotted near the origin, then consumers view that experience as subpar. If the store experience scores high, like a Sephora would, that rating would be plotted as further away from the origin.

However, it is difficult for consumers to evaluate retailers in the abstract. It is much easier for them to determine whether a retailer is above or below their expectations for value for each dimension. Therefore, before we plot a retailer's score on each dimension, we need to anticipate what the consumers' threshold expectations are: What is the fair value or bare minimum that a retailer has to deliver to be considered acceptable by the consumer on each of the four axes? Anything that falls below that threshold would be considered inferior performance—and retailers cannot survive in a competitive marketplace with inferior performance. For example, RadioShack stores were below customer threshold expectations on several of the dimensions, and as a result, the retailer went bankrupt.

In Figure 1.3, these fair-value expectations are plotted as hash marks on each axis. The customers' expectations are all drawn equidistant from the origin, but this does not have to be the case. The further out the customers' threshold expectations are from the ori-

Figure 1.3. The Kahn Retailing Success Matrix: Plotting a Competitive Position

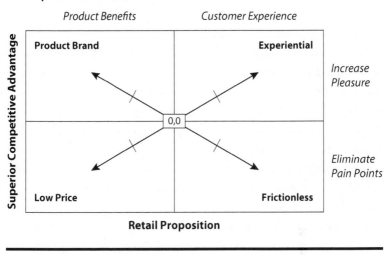

gin, the higher the expectations are on that dimension, representing a more competitively difficult market in which to compete and win. To measure these fair-value thresholds, dedicated market research should be conducted to see what consumers are expecting. For more on fair-value threshold measurement, please see the appendix.

After the customer expectations are plotted, then the firm's own position can be plotted on these axes, relative to these fair-value or threshold expectations. Is the firm delivering below or above customers' expectations on each of these dimensions?

Ever-Changing Customer Expectations

To survive, retailers must aspire to be at least at fair value in all of the quadrants. But to be a market leader, retailers must provide *superior* value—and literally be the best if possible—in at least one quadrant. In addition, in competitive markets, it is necessary to be tops in two of the quadrants.

If each of the retailing titans strives for leadership positions and offer superior value above and beyond customers' threshold expectations on any specific dimension, this will inevitably shape what customers come to expect and, in time, demand. As each retailer strives to win and offers something of ever-greater value to the customer, this new advantage becomes the new standard for fair value—and the new expected requirement to compete effectively.

For example, when a particular retailer makes the commitment to offer two-day delivery—or even same-day delivery—the expectations as to what is fair value in delivery timing ratchet up. Thus, as the industry becomes more competitive, customers' expectations move further and further out to the corners of the grid, and it becomes more difficult to compete. Amazon has raised customers' expectations as to what should be expected from a frictionless shopping experience. Sephora has proven that customers want to interact and sample its beauty products themselves and are no longer content to wait for a sales associate to pull the product out from behind the counter.

Therefore, to be competitive in the market, retailers have to constantly keep track of customer expectations and make sure they are at least delivering value up to what is needed. This is forever challenging because these expectations are constantly increasing if the competition is actively trying to take over as market leader.

Winning Leadership Strategies

The final step here is to plot out a winning strategy. In the very competitive world of retail, a winning strategy requires leadership in one quadrant that is then leveraged to provide leadership in a second quadrant. This requires maniacal focus on one's strengths and on developing business models that pave the way to dominance.

Historically, strategic frameworks such as Treacy and Wiersema's *The Discipline of Market Leaders* have suggested that market leaders should be the best at *one* thing, and then good enough at everything else, to win customers over. The argument was that if firms tried to be good at everything, they would not succeed, and would end up being "not good enough" at anything or "stuck in the middle," whereas those firms that focused on one strategy would end up with a leadership position.

However, given the ruthless leadership and disruption of the retailing industry that has come about through Amazon's dominance, I would argue that being the best at one value discipline is now insufficient. Retailers must build on their initial strengths to win on at least one other dimension—while also not ignoring the rest.

In the nonleadership quadrants, companies must deliver only up to customers' fair-value expectations. In other words, in these other dimensions "good enough" will often suffice. Indeed, I believe retailers should actually be wary of trying to be more than "good enough" on the nondominant quadrants because these efforts could strain resources that would be better directed at the leadership strengths.

Since all customers are different and have different value priorities, some will be attracted to different retailers depending upon the customer's unique needs. The choice of which strategy to pursue should depend on the firm's historic strengths, where it believes it can offer a significant differential competitive value·over and above what the competition can deliver, as well as the various weights different customer segments apply to each of the dimensions. Notably, some customer segments may be more lucrative than others. Leadership depends on offering superior value in two quadrants and meeting fair value in the other two. But offering fair value in the nondominant quadrants can be challenging because customers' expectations are constantly increasing as they learn what retailing leaders are willing to offer.

The importance of the relative dimensions will vary by retailing vertical and by customer segment. Further, movements along the axes may have different cost profiles. Plotting one's positions and your competitors' positions over time, as well as recording changing customer expectations, will provide a dynamic map for keeping track of market performance.

Going back to the examples at the start of this chapter and plotting those retailing leaders' strategies on the grid provides proof that companies must become leaders by winning in two quadrants. These two-quadrant winning strategies are illustrated in Figure 1.4. Amazon and Walmart are both trying to be leaders by removing pain points from both the product and customer experience; however, they start from different strengths. Warby Parker leverages its strong brand name to gain customers but would probably not be successful if it did not also offer a lower-price advantage. That is similarly the case with Zara. Sephora builds on its superior customer loyalty programs to offer unparalleled customer experiences in its stores. Luxury brands have learned that offering top branded products is not suf-

Figure 1.4. Two-Quadrant Winning Strategies

Amazon

Product Brand	Experiential
Low Price ◄———	Frictionless

Walmart

Product Brand	Experiential
Low Price ———►	Frictionless

Warby Parker, Zara

Product Brand	Experiential
Low Price ▼	Frictionless

T.J.Maxx, Costco, Luxury, Sephora

Product Brand ——►▲	Experiential
Low Price ⟋	Frictionless

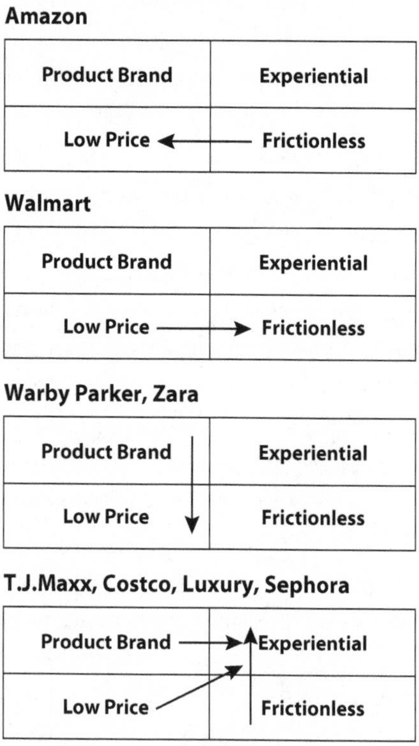

ficient; they also must follow through with luxurious customer experiences. Costco and T.J.Maxx do not merely rely on low price but also offer a treasure hunt experience to lure customers into their stores.

Conclusion

The retailing industry is very competitive, and new technologies are disrupting old models at a frantic pace. Successful retailers must constantly monitor their competitors and track changing consumer demands and expectations. The Kahn Retailing Success Matrix suggests the way for retailers to win in such a challenging marketplace is to be the leader in one of the four quadrants and to build on this strength to catch up to the leaders in a second quadrant. This is illustrated in the "arrow" strategy, depicted in Figure 1.4.

The model does not suggest that the other two quadrants should be ignored, but it is impossible to be the best at everything. It is only necessary to compete at fair value in these two quadrants, rather than looking for a leadership position.

A company's choice in strategy will depend upon that retailers' inherent strengths and the culture of the organization, and ultimately will set priorities for future allocation of resources. Customers are attracted to different retailers depending upon their own needs, so the choice of strategy will inevitably attract specific customer segments— and, by extension, inevitably turn away others.

The Kahn Retailing Success Matrix provides a graphing mechanism that allows changes in marketplace dynamics to be recorded over time. In the chapters that follow, I will use this framework to plot various successful retailers' strategies. I won't be using actual data to plot these strategies, but rather will use the tool as a way to communicate the strategic choices simply and clearly.

Chapter 2

Amazon the Disruptor: Laser Focus on Customer Convenience

In This Chapter: Kahn Retailing Success Strategy
- Key Leadership Strength: Frictionless, Pain-Free, Convenient Customer Experience
- Secondary Leadership Strength: Low-Price Leader
- Fair Value in Branded Product and Experiential Quadrants

If Walmart was the retailing juggernaut of the 1990s, there is no question that Amazon holds that title today. And the difference in what Amazon is doing as compared to what everyone else is doing is probably even more extreme than the era in which Walmart essentially put America's mom-and-pop retailers out of business. It is not an exaggeration to say that Amazon has fundamentally changed the shopping experience.

The numbers verify these claims. In 2015 Amazon's market cap became more valuable than Walmart's. Amazon's revenues in September 2017 were just under $44 billion, and it is the number one internet retailer in the United States, with 34% of the market. Experts' estimates are that its share could increase to 50% by 2021.

Although the retailer with the highest overall retail sales (both online and offline) is still Walmart, Amazon carries 30 times the SKUs of Walmart and is the top online seller in Europe and Japan. Amazon is also strong in India, which it entered only in 2013 (by contrast, the company is still lagging in China because of the fierce competition from Alibaba and JD.com). Putting all of this together, experts forecast that Amazon would be the number two retailer in the world within the next five years.

Amazon's stated mission is to be the Earth's most customer-centric company—offering the best price, with the largest selection, and the fastest delivery. To achieve this goal, Amazon continually reinvests profits in R&D, and has repeatedly turned out state-of-the-art innovations that attract more and more customers to its platform.

Amazon's Beginnings

Amazon started in 1995 as an online bookstore offering customers the opportunity to order books anytime, anywhere, with the largest assortment of titles that could be found anywhere. Jeff Bezos chose the book industry specifically because the product could be digitalized so that the online assortment could be enormous—bigger, Bezos knew, than any physical store could ever match. Unlike other retail websites operating at the time, Amazon's website made it as easy to "browse" online as it might be in a physical store. Customers could see the front cover, back cover, and some of the inside materials, as well as access other customers' reviews, interviews with the authors, and related book titles.

The majority of the books were priced 10% to 30% cheaper than those sold at other stores, and customers did not pay sales tax for purchases made online. These advantages impressed customers and resulted in powerful word-of-mouth recommendations, which eventually spurred exponential growth. In December of 1995, just 2,200 people had ever visited Amazon's webpage; by the spring of 1997, more than 80,000 had come on board. From books, Amazon then moved on to other digitizable products such as music and DVDs. Amazon's success, and its innovative platform, soon put one of the world's largest big-box book retailers, Borders, completely out of business.

Amazon Marketplace

In 2000 Amazon began allowing outside companies, including its direct competitors (in terms of products sold), to sell their wares on an Amazon open e-commerce platform called Amazon Marketplace. Amazon collected a sales commission of up to 5% of each sale. In exchange for this fee, Amazon would deliver and store the product for the merchant and allow consumers to buy the products using Amazon's purchase technology.

Brands and other retailers including Toys "R" Us, Target, Circuit City, Gap, and Lands' End quickly signed on, only bolstering Amazon's grip on the marketplace. The program not only allowed Amazon to offer the largest assortment available online, but, as will be discussed later, it also served to provide a sizable source of profit. With this innovation, Amazon was soon selling every product from A to Z, as its logo promised. Amazon Marketplace now accounts for about half of products sold on the Amazon platform.

Amazon Web Services

When working with the retailers on Amazon Marketplace, Amazon recognized that each merchant's IT application deployment required a long development process to build databases, computing, payment processing, and storage components. Each retailer had to start from scratch and go through similar processes, resulting in great inefficiencies.

Amazon then entered the Infrastructure as a Service (IaaS) business by utilizing the advantages of cloud computing and building up a reliable, scalable, and cost-efficient IT infrastructure called Amazon Web Services (AWS). Pricing was like a utility; users paid for what they used, thus avoiding costly upfront costs to build up systems.

AWS has been hugely successful. Small developers who could not afford the upfront development costs signed on to AWS for cost-effective and reliable service. By 2015 AWS was servicing more than

1 million customers in 190 countries. It quickly became the dominant player in the space, with revenues larger than all of its competitors combined. AWS today offers over 70 IT services including networking, storage, and analytics.

Plotting Amazon's Retailing Strategy

Amazon is definitely more than just a retailing company; it is also a true force in logistics, consumer technology, cloud computing, and media and entertainment. But its many moving parts work together to reinforce its dominant position in retailing—and that is the perspective that I will focus on here in discussing Amazon. This idea was reinforced in conversations that *Harvard Business Review* senior editors had with Jeff Bezos about the importance of his consumer-facing business (i.e., retail). The following is an excerpt from those interviews:

> When I'm talking with people outside the company, there's a question that comes up very commonly: "What's going to change in the next five to ten years?" But I very rarely get asked "What's not going to change in the next five to ten years?" . . . For our business, most of [what I'm counting on not to change turns] out to be customer insights. Look at what's important to the customers in our consumer-facing business. They want selection, low prices, and fast delivery. This can be different from business to business: There are companies serving other customers who wouldn't put price, for example, in that set. But having found out what those things are for our customers, I can't imagine that ten years from now they are going to say, "I love Amazon, but if only they could deliver my products a little more slowly." And they're not going to, ten years from now, say, "I really love Amazon, but I wish their prices were a little higher." So we know that when we put energy into defect reduction, which reduces our cost structure and thereby allows lower prices, that will be paying us dividends ten years from now. If we keep putting energy into that flywheel, ten years from now it'll be spinning faster and faster.

To discuss Amazon's retailing strategy, I will use the Kahn Retailing Success Matrix as a framework. According to the framework, a leadership strategy in retailing requires the firm to be the market leader in one quadrant, build on that advantage to achieve leadership in a second quadrant, and then maintain fair value in the other two quadrants.

Amazon seems to be following this prescription. It is clearly the market leader in the Frictionless quadrant. It builds on that advantage to be the market leader in a second quadrant (Low Price). Finally, Amazon is ready to provide at least fair value on customer expectations in the remaining two quadrants (Product Brand and Experiential).

Specifically, as Figure 2.1 shows, in the Frictionless quadrant Amazon is pushing consumers' expectations higher and higher, and constantly finds itself ahead of the pack. Other retailers scramble to try and keep up as Amazon keeps investing in R&D and developing innovations that allow it to continually leapfrog the competition.

In the Low Price quadrant, Amazon's strategy is to fiercely compete and to offer the lowest price possible. Amazon subsidizes thin margins in its retail transactions by leveraging profitability in other parts of its business, such as AWS, Marketplace, and Amazon Prime.

In the Product Brand quadrant, Amazon is not a leader, but it scrambles to offer products and brands consumers want on its platform. In addition, Amazon tries to mitigate other brands' advantages by convincing consumers that those brands' premium prices are not warranted. This is illustrated on the matrix by showing the movement of the fair-value line downward toward the origin in this quadrant. This, then, allows Amazon to compete effectively either with its own brands or with those outside offered on Amazon Marketplace.

Finally, in the Experiential quadrant, Amazon is currently below fair value, but with the development of its own stores and the purchase of Whole Foods it is preparing to compete effectively in offline retailing while continuing to be the leader in online retailing. These strategies are plotted in Figure 2.1, and will be discussed in more detail in the next sections.

Figure 2.1. Plotting Amazon on the Kahn Retailing Success Matrix

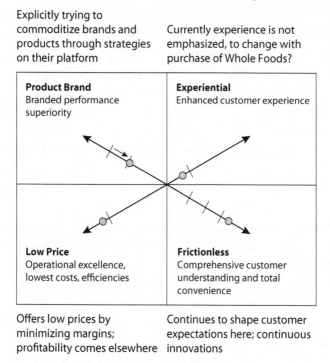

Explicitly trying to commoditize brands and products through strategies on their platform	Currently experience is not emphasized, to change with purchase of Whole Foods?
Product Brand Branded performance superiority	**Experiential** Enhanced customer experience
Low Price Operational excellence, lowest costs, efficiencies	**Frictionless** Comprehensive customer understanding and total convenience
Offers low prices by minimizing margins; profitability comes elsewhere	Continues to shape customer expectations here; continuous innovations

Key Leadership Position: Frictionless, Pain-Free Customer Experience

At Amazon, we are committed to being the most customer-centric company on Earth.

—Amazon.com

Amazon's defining leadership strategy is to be the best in the world in the Frictionless quadrant, and it achieves this by constantly innovating and raising customer expectations as to what it means to enjoy a convenient, seamless shopping experience. Amazon is laser focused on customer experience, specifically in terms of eliminating any pain points and proactively giving customers what they desire. As Bezos says: "Customers are always beautifully, wonderfully dissatisfied, even when they report being happy and business is great. Even when they don't yet know it, customers want something better, and your desire to delight customers will drive you to invent on their behalf."

One of Amazon's earliest innovations, "1-Click," was introduced in 1997, and it serves as a metaphor for Amazon's overarching philosophy that shopping should be as easy and convenient as possible. "1-Click" shopping meant that once consumers had entered in their personal payment information, they did not have to enter it in again; rather a simple click on the desired item would purchase it. This idea was so novel at the time that Amazon was awarded a US patent for the technology (notably, the patent expired in 2017). It is hard now to imagine that this was a patentable idea, but in fact Bezos sued Barnes & Noble in 1999. He won, and Barnes & Noble was forced to add an extra step to its checkout process.

Amazon's hugely popular loyalty program, Amazon Prime, provides the company with another opportunity for success in this quadrant, by providing the ability to collect customer data and to use this data not only to fulfill customers' current needs, but also, importantly, to anticipate customers' *future* needs. Finally, the always forward-looking Amazon is looking to be a leader in the burgeoning world of the "connected home," otherwise known as the Internet of Things (IoT). With the introduction of Amazon Echo, Amazon appears to have developed another source of data and opportunities that will allow it to interact even further with consumers.

Best Loyalty Program: Amazon Prime

In 2005 Amazon launched its loyalty program, Amazon Prime. Initially, members were charged a $79 annual fee (the annual fee jumped to $99 in 2013, and the monthly fee increased to $12.99 per month from $10.99 in 2018). This fee guaranteed unlimited two-day shipping and a discounted rate for overnight shipping—and there was a good reason why. Shipping costs, delivery delays, and other hassles were the single biggest impediment to online shopping at the time, and Amazon Prime effectively removed them from the Amazon experience.

In 2011 Amazon offered even further perks to its Prime members, including Instant Video, the Kindle Lending Library, Prime Music, Prime Drive, and Prime Photo. Other benefits include one-hour restaurant delivery, one free ebook a month, ad-free viewing of a video-game channel, and access to streaming media content including new content that Amazon studios is developing. In addition, Prime members have access to Amazon's best price deals. All of these factors make Amazon Prime members exceedingly loyal. It also provides Amazon with many touchpoints with the consumer each day, and each of these touchpoints provides more data.

Amazon aggressively recruits new customers to become Prime members. For example, it gives students a free six-month subscription to Amazon Prime. When I was teaching the marketing core to Wharton MBA students in 2017, every single student in my classes had signed on for the free Amazon trial, and 100% of them said they were going to remain subscribed when the trial ended. In 2015 Amazon created "Prime Day" to celebrate its 20th anniversary. During this one-day-only event, Prime members were offered hugely discounted items for sale. The event generated 86.3 million visits; for comparison, the company saw 87.1 million visits on Black Friday and 95.3 million visits on Cyber Monday during the same time period.

Strategies such as these continue to help Amazon attract new Prime customers, and as of 2017 the company had 80 million subscribers in total. Additionally, 64% of all American households had at least one Prime account. This matters, it turns out, because Prime members spend 40% to 68% more money on Amazon's site than nonmembers do, with the higher percentages occurring for customers who have been members longer. Amazon Prime membership also encourages much more frequent shopping. According to one survey done by an independent consumer research firm, 95% of Prime members planned to renew their membership and renewed members spend more in the subsequent year than they had in the previous year. Bezos calls Prime the company's "flywheel"—

a device used in engines to provide constant energy. Prime keeps customers loyal to Amazon and accelerates their purchasing, and this ever-spinning engine primes other aspects of the business.

Strategic Use of Data

Amazon's algorithms help provide personalized communications and recommendations for customers, and its detailed search filters help those customers find exactly what they want, when they want it. The more customers Amazon entices to Prime, the more likely sellers are to sign on to Marketplace and to use AWS. As a result, Amazon not only has an extensive dataset on how consumers search, purchase, and consume, but it also has data from its Marketplace that show how sellers sell, and from AWS it learns how developers create their infrastructure and retailing support systems. With this information, Amazon can not only provide the best recommendations for consumers but can also use state-of-the art innovations to maximize its logistics and technology-enriched environments. This strategy of getting data from all sources, and then leveraging it to get smarter products that entice more consumers and sellers to its site, is yet another example of the classic flywheel model.

Connected Home: Amazon and the IoT

Underlying the fast-growing world of the IoT is the idea that computers and other digital devices can transfer data over a network without requiring human-to-human or human-to-computer interaction. We are in the early stages of this burgeoning market, but Amazon has begun to lay the groundwork for dominance there too. One of its early plays in the spirit of IoT was the Amazon Dash Wand. Introduced in 2014 and offered free to Prime users, the Dash Wand barcode scanner allowed Prime users to scan grocery items in their homes and order them immediately through Amazon Fresh.

Soon after, in 2015, Amazon introduced Dash Buttons, which were also given to Prime customers for free. The Dash Button was a

"1-Click" ordering button that was branded and could be used similarly to the Dash Wand to order immediate delivery of specific branded products. The Dash Buttons were developed for consumer packaged good categories such cleaning products, toilet paper, juice, and dog food.

Voice-Activated Smart Speakers: Amazon Echo

A major emphasis in the IoT, or connected home space, is the growing focus on voice assistants that allow for a customer-centric purchase journey right in the home. Amazon's entry here is the Amazon Echo, a voice-enabled wireless speaker that answers to commands beginning with the word "Alexa." If Amazon can get Echo in the majority of US homes, it will become the dominant platform for natural language processing interaction—connecting the home, wearables, and even the car dashboard.

Amazon controls about 70% of the market for voice-activated smart speakers. During the Thanksgiving shopping period in 2017, which Amazon called "Turkey 5" (representing the five shopping days from Thanksgiving Thursday to Cyber Monday), Amazon aggressively priced its Echo and Echo Dot speakers to get more and more devices into the homes of new and existing customers (industry experts estimated that Amazon was selling Alexa hardware at a 10% to 20% net loss). Gartner is reporting that virtual assistants will be the dominant source of interaction between shoppers and retailers by 2020.

It remains to be seen how well Amazon will succeed here, as it is facing tough competition in Google (Home), which has recently partnered with Walmart, and Apple's Siri. However, early data are showing that 40% of people who interact with Alexa shop more with Amazon. eMarketer released a forecast for 2017 and onward estimating that almost 6 million Americans would be using a voice-activated assistant device at least once a month, with the largest market share going to Amazon's Echo. Another study from Juniper Research predicts that smart speakers will be installed in over 70 million households by 2022, or 55% of all homes nationwide.

Plans for the Future? *Amazon-Sears Deal*

In 2017 Amazon announced it was partnering with Sears to distribute its Kenmore-branded appliances. Although some believe that Sears as a retailer has seen better days, its Kenmore brand is still one of the most respected brands in the appliance industry. With this partnership, consumers will be able to purchase these appliance brands directly through Amazon's site, while Amazon will gain access to Sears's industry knowledge, including logistics and distribution expertise. One of Amazon's goals with Alexa is to have consumers control thermostats, lamps, and other connected devices in the home through voice commands. Access to a slew of appliances suggests Amazon envisions a future that will see more control through voice commands of all appliances in the home.

In addition to the very public announcement of the Sears partnership, Amazon has more quietly made other investments in companies that suggest its growing interest in artificial intelligence and smart home voice controls. For example, it has invested in small tech companies making connected sprinkler systems, connected intercom systems, smart pet feeders, and security cameras. The intention would be to connect all of these things, or things like these, into its Alexa ecosystem.

And Amazon may ultimately provide Echo with more advanced capabilities as well. The company recently added a camera to Echo, giving Alexa the ability to "see." Is the next step to add gesture tracking capabilities, virtual reality, and more advanced language processing abilities?

Putting all of these pieces together, the dream of an effective IoT seems closer than ever. All of these innovations make it clear that Amazon is far and away the leader in the Frictionless quadrant. Next, we discuss how Amazon can build on this advantage to become the low-price leader as well.

Building on Customer Centricity to Become a Low-Price Leader

Everybody wants . . . low prices. . . . [T]hat is something that is universally desired all over the world.

—Jeff Bezos

Amazon is definitely a low-price leader, both for its own brands and for the outside brands offered for sale on its site. Amazon can afford to trim margins on its own brands because retail transactions are not its critical profit generator. Rather, profit generation comes through its AWS, Amazon Prime, and Amazon Marketplace initiatives: AWS and Amazon Marketplace generate profits through the pockets of Amazon's competitors, while Prime generates profits through subscription fees and increased purchasing from its loyal members. The low-price strategies that are encouraged through Amazon's strategies described in this chapter (in addition to the superb customer service and convenience) keep Amazon's customers addicted to the site.

Also, it's important to note that while Amazon is a public company, Wall Street has for years allowed Amazon to focus on a long-term perspective—a stark contrast to the short-term, quarterly scrutiny that other retailers have to face. This allows Amazon to continually invest in R&D fulfillment capabilities to improve the customer experience.

In addition to promoting pricing strategies that encourage intense price competition, Amazon also works to improve margins by efficiency in its cost structure. This is accomplished through Amazon's automated fulfillment centers that can efficiently and quickly move product from warehouses to where they need to be delivered (by plane or cargo trucks).

Profits Come from Other Services: AWS, Marketplace, Prime

Rather than trying to make significant profit on each retail transaction (according to one expert I spoke with, Amazon has 3% margins on its merchandise transactions), Amazon is profitable through three mechanisms: (1) AWS, (2) Amazon Prime, which provides Amazon with revenues through a subscription model and increased spending, and (3) Amazon Marketplace.

AWS in particular may be the engine behind Amazon's profits, as it provides much-desired server capacity to small retailers and startups. In 2015 Amazon offered details on AWS's financial performance, stating at the time that AWS had generated $7.9 billion in revenues—7.4% of Amazon's total revenues—and $1.9 billion in operating income, or 41% of its total operating income. Amazon reported that AWS made $17 billion in revenue in 2017. According to ZDNet, the majority of Amazon's 2017 operating income came from AWS.

Amazon Prime is also a revenue generator for the company, although executives do not offer any concrete numbers here. Various studies put Amazon's Prime membership base at between 63 million and 69 million, and a Morgan Stanley survey found 40% of Prime members spend more than $1,000 a year via Amazon. Some estimates suggest that Prime sales represent 60% of the total dollar value of all merchandise sold on the site. Amazon has only publically acknowledged that Prime members spend more and shop across a greater number of categories than the other shoppers on Amazon.

Amazon Marketplace also generates strong margins selling for the company, even though Amazon does not own any of the products sold there; this platform essentially ensures that Amazon's hand is in all of its competitors' transactions that are made on its site. For these third-party sales, Amazon charges fees and does not have to take on inventory risks. In 2017 these sales represented nearly a fifth of Amazon's total revenue.

To further serve these third-party sellers, Amazon offers Fulfillment by Amazon (FBA), where vendors (for a fee, of course) can use Amazon's fulfillment centers for warehousing, order fulfillment, logistics, and customer service. These products are also then allowed to be offered in Amazon's Prime program, which offers its customers free two-day shipping. According to Amazon, participation in the FBA program increases sales by more than 20%. Interestingly (in terms of profitability for Amazon), it costs third-party sellers *more* to sell on Amazon with FBA than on eBay. However, more logistics options are available, and even accounting for the higher fees, Amazon's business with third-party sellers is growing.

Marketplace Tactics Drive Merchants to Lower-Price Strategies

In addition to being a profit generator for the company, Amazon Marketplace also incentivizes merchants to lower prices. First, since Marketplace is an open platform, Amazon does not police it to make sure that diverted gray market products are not included. Amazon's open platform allows almost anyone to create new product listings. Consequently, products can be sold by resellers unbeknownst to the manufacturers, and the products may violate contracts. For example, the third-party sellers typically buy legitimate product from big-box retailers such as Walmart or T.J.Maxx, or even the brands' own outlets, and then these resellers offer those brands for sale on Amazon with slightly higher prices than they acquired them for. These products can easily then be sold below the minimum advertised prices—and they may be sold under brand names that are not quite legitimate.

Second, if a product can come in at the most competitive price, it will be labeled with Amazon's "Buy Box," which will increase sales volume enormously, compensating for lower margins and providing more commission to Amazon. This encourages overall price competition among Amazon's competitors, which helps make Amazon the go-to lower-priced retailer.

Third, for product searches that occur on other search engines, Amazon buys display advertising for popular brands, and then sends those consumers back to the Amazon site. Since Amazon has access to the third-party purchase transactions that occur on its site, it can make sure it prioritizes this display advertising to feature brands that have been shown to attract consumers. Once on the Amazon site, the customer is subject to Amazon algorithms and website priorities that encourage price competition. In addition, Amazon uses this valuable information to offer its own lower-priced alternatives in the Amazon Basics program.

Another interesting strategy that Amazon is using to ensure that it will be able to offer the lowest prices is to partner with merchants in India who will be able to sell their goods directly to US consumers on the Amazon platform. Amazon is partnering with India behemoths like the Tata Group as well as smaller peddlers who can offer handcrafted goods. In addition to broadening its product line, Amazon can, via this new initiative, tack on large margins. Bezos has said he will prioritize India e-commerce as an avenue for growth for the future. At the same time, Amazon may be looking toward the Middle East: In 2017 it purchased Souq.com, known as the "Amazon of the Middle East." This potentially opens up Egypt, Saudi Arabia, and the United Arab Emirates to Amazon as well.

Finally, Amazon competes against the third-party merchants that sell on its platform with its own private brand called Amazon Basics. Many of the products in this category are sold only to Prime members. Again, since Amazon controls all the data, it has enormous insight into where there may be gaps for lower-priced brands, and then can produce those private-label products. Amazon currently has private-label brands in apparel, consumer packaged goods, and diapers. The company also makes it hard for other retailers to match its prices, as it has begun to use blocking technology so the retailers cannot see what is happening with regard to Amazon's branded product efforts.

In spite of these aggressive tactics designed to lower prices, brands and resellers are enticed to sell on Amazon Marketplace because they do not have to spend marketing dollars to drive traffic to their site; Amazon's volume is bigger than any other e-commerce site. And 55% of product searches in the United States start on Amazon, as compared to 28% on other search engines such as Google.

Efficiency in Lowest Cost Fulfillment: Amazon's Fulfillment Centers

Another way Amazon maintains its low price structure is through cost containment. Amazon is on target to fulfill its mission of becoming a logistics and transport leader, which is key to retail dominance.

It can make a wider range of products available and deliver those products faster than its competitors can. Some of this expertise in logistics has come from its hiring a number of Walmart executives to leverage that retailer's expertise.

Typically, at the fulfillment centers trucks deliver boxes where they are photographed and scanned on all sides. In order to make it easier for truck drivers to pick up and drop off packages at warehouses, Amazon has launched an app called "Relay" that gives Amazon direct access to millions of truck drivers across the United States. The Relay app allows truck drivers to use a QR code to get through security so that they do not have to manually go through the security gates. It's kind of like an E-ZPass for truck drivers. This is the first step toward total automation of the truck delivery process and is critical because almost 80% of all cargo in the United States is delivered via trucks.

Once at the fulfillment centers, algorithms, robots, and driverless vehicles are then utilized to sort each parcel automatically and direct them to where they need to go. This can now be done in half the time it took humans with barcode scanners to do it. (Although highly automated, these fulfillment centers still need human workers for oversight and boxing.)

Products that leave the warehouse are delivered via air and cargo trailers, and plans are already in place to eventually use Amazon delivery drones. Amazon has strengthened its air delivery system by purchasing cargo planes for its Prime Air service, making it less dependent on more traditional shippers like FedEx, DHL, and USPS. Amazon also manages its delivery system partly by its creation of Flex, which is an Uber-like system of independent drivers.

The demand for faster and faster delivery times has necessitated that Amazon expand its footprint of fulfillment and distribution centers, building them closer to where the customer lives. Because Amazon does not have the physical store presence of its competition, the company's leadership have been strategically locating its warehouses. Originally, these warehouse were located in states without sales tax, but the strategy changed more recently to allow Amazon to offer same-day delivery to more of its customers. In 2015 it was estimated that Amazon could easily serve almost 30% of its customers with same-day delivery service. Amazon is also aggressively building fulfillment centers in Europe and Asia.

Maintaining Fair Value in the Branded Products Quadrant

> *Your margin is my opportunity.*
> —One of Jeff Bezos's "best-known bon mots,"
> according to the *Wall Street Journal*

While Amazon's critical leadership advantages are in the Frictionless and Low Price quadrants, it must maintain a credible presence in the Product Brand quadrant as well—offering at least fair value here. For sure, it is able to compete effectively by offering the largest breadth of assortment, and, as described, it has been able to bring in a significant number of branded products to its platform through Amazon Marketplace.

But producers of many of the most prestigious branded products (which consumers really covet) are loath to sell through Amazon, because they know they would be putting too much control into Amazon's hands. Amazon will dictate inventory, control the customer data, and set pricing. Although Amazon will sell some customer analytics to the brand, it will not release information on conversion rates and customer demographics. Further, Amazon's algorithms prioritize Amazon's goals—not the brands' goals.

Therefore, Amazon's strategy is not helping it to be the leader in offering prestigious, luxury brands. Rather, as noted, Jeff Bezos's strategy seems to be to try to commoditize those brands, and then use Amazon Prime advantages to incentivize consumers to purchase from Amazon Basics (on price value) or from Amazon Marketplace, where website algorithms also encourage lower pricing, rather than having them purchase premium-priced branded goods from other competitors. Hence brands' margins are Amazon's opportunity. And again, this was plotted on the matrix by showing movement of the fair-value line toward the origin.

Although it is not Amazon's mission to build the reputation of premium-priced and luxury brands, Amazon does care about its own brand. Bezos has been quoted as saying, "You can have the best technology, you can have the best business model, but if the storytelling isn't amazing, it won't matter. . . . Nobody will watch." Various public relations activities and some spending on digital marketing helped raise awareness for Amazon. As it grew, word of mouth, a multitude of articles and books, as well as Bezos himself helped build the Amazon brand. In 2018 Amazon also created a Super Bowl ad featuring its Alexa product, and Jeff Bezos appeared in the commercial.

Goal to Offer Largest Breadth of Assortment; Brands' Equity Often Diminished as a Result

In order to offer the largest assortment possible, Amazon encourages third-party retailers to sell on Amazon through a variety of inducements. As stated, Amazon does not police its offerings, and as such these third-party sellers may be selling branded products in ways that are not appreciated by the brands themselves. Further, Amazon does not regularly police counterfeiters; Amazon maintains that is the brand's responsibility.

Given Amazon's strategies, it is clear that although Amazon may be customer-centric, it is not competitor-merchant friendly—even though these merchants are incentivized to sell on the Amazon platform. When merchants sell on Amazon, they don't own their own data; they are always incentivized to compete on price (thus cannibalizing their own potentially higher-margin business that could have come through direct selling or through selling on other retailers' platforms); and they can't offer a customized high-touch customer experience, which is crucial to some brands' cache. While Amazon's website is functional for sure, aesthetically beautiful it is not.

Why Do Some Brands Agree to Sell on Amazon?

Given Amazon's strategies to promote lower and lower prices, why would retailers or brands sell on Amazon Marketplace in the first place? If the brand is small enough, there is a big attraction to get access to Amazon's volume, without having to spend marketing dollars to drive traffic to its site. For very small brands, this may be the only way for them to get scale.

But even big retailers like Toys "R" Us have been attracted to Amazon . . . and ultimately suffered for the relationship. In 2000 Amazon and Toys "R" Us signed a 10-year partnership that made Amazon the exclusive online retailer for Toys "R" Us products. Amazon designed the website and assisted in warehouse, fulfillment, and customer service. Customers who went to the Toys "R" Us website put their orders into an Amazon shopping cart.

Why did Toys "R" Us do this? Apparently, it had the mistaken impression that it would be the exclusive provider of toys for Amazon. But Amazon had other ideas, as it also partnered with Target and other independent third-party sellers to sell toys. Toys "R" Us filed a lawsuit against Amazon and in 2006 a judge ordered the dissolution of the partnership. Amazon was deemed to have broken the contract but was not forced to pay any damages, and continued to have success in the toy business. Toys "R" Us, on the other hand, had to play catch-up in order to become a successful online retailer. In 2017 it declared bankruptcy.

Amazon is ruthless in leveraging its connections and competing against branded products that are popular with its customers—and many times brands are helpless to stop them. For example, Amazon went up against Lululemon in 2017 by using a top Lululemon supplier, Eclat Textile, to make a private-label athletic clothing for Amazon. This allowed Amazon to tap into Lululemon's signature Luon fabric as well as newer materials. Although Lulu has some patents, most of them focus on design features and not fabric technology. Lulu's share price dropped two days after the news was reported.

Amazon has also been relentless in competing against book publishers in its quest to cater to its customers' interests first. For example, Amazon makes it very easy for consumers to choose to buy a used book rather than a new book by making them seem virtually the same. However, when the consumer chooses to buy the used book, the publisher makes nothing—but Amazon does. The value of the used book, though, is a function of the investment the publisher and author made in producing the original content. Under Amazon's model there is no royalty or any profit stream when the product is resold.

Is there anything a brand can do to protect itself? The brand can enforce an online reseller policy with strict language that forbids distributors from reselling unsold inventory to unauthorized resellers. They would, however, have to scrupulously police this themselves.

Why Do Big Brands with Strong Brand Equity Capitulate?

Given Amazon's stated strategy to not protect brands from counterfeits and its desire to continually lower prices, why would brands with strong brand equity and status agree to sell on Amazon? To understand this, a good example is Nike.

For more than 20 years, Nike refused to sell its products on Amazon. But then, in June 2017, Nike made the announcement that it had reversed its decision and agreed to sell its products on the e-commerce site. Why?

First of all, even though historically Nike hadn't agreed to officially sell its products on Amazon, many third-party retailers were already selling legitimate Nike products there, and Nike had no control over those transactions or pricing strategies. In fact, according to a Morgan Stanley survey, even though Nike did not sanction sales of its product on Amazon, Nike was the most purchased apparel brand on the site!

Further, as noted, more than 50% of consumers' online product search begins on Amazon. That means if Nike is not *officially* present there, it has a high likelihood of losing those sales, particularly among Amazon Prime customers who are extremely loyal to Amazon. Third, many of Nike's competitors were already on Amazon: Adidas added Amazon as a distributor in 2014, and Under Armour and TaylorMade have also signed on. Having its competitors on Amazon as Amazon became the go-to e-commerce site for sportswear and athleisure products ultimately made Nike vulnerable to the possibility that its loyal Nike customers would defect.

Understandably, then, Nike decided that it had to take the upper hand with regard to Amazon and protect its brand. Unlike other brands, Nike has enormous brand equity, so it was able to negotiate a deal with Amazon whereby they got more channel control. In the deal, Amazon agreed to police the Nike brand on Marketplace with stricter policies about counterfeits, and also provided restrictions on sales that Nike does not sanction. Even with these concessions, Nike remains concerned as Amazon sells its products but does little to build its brand. In return, Nike product is officially available on Amazon. Thus, Nike's strong brand equity will now help bring *even more* customers to the Amazon platform. Obviously, this makes Amazon stronger and continues to erode the attraction of traditional retailers. The handwriting seems to be on the wall: In a spring 2017 Cowen survey, Amazon equaled Foot Locker as the preferred US retailer for buying sneakers.

Nike might just be the beginning of a flood of premium and luxury brands realizing the power of Amazon. After the Nike deal, Amazon signed an agreement with Violet Grey that will allow Amazon to offer its luxury beauty brands on its site. Many big brands are still reluctant; Birkenstock's CEO has taken a strong stand against Amazon, even as Amazon solicits third-party retailers to break their sales agreements with Birkenstock and offer their products for sale on Amazon. The Birkenstock CEO characterized Amazon's actions as "unconscionable" and "pathetic."

If a brand is strong enough, as Nike proved, it may have some clout to get Amazon to respond. In August 2016, Amazon introduced a "brand gating" program that prohibited some third-party merchants from selling established brands such as Microsoft and Burberry. But only some brands (presumably, those brands with enough clout) are on this list, and companies that are not listed will still fall prey to unauthorized sellers.

Moving into Fashion

Although Amazon's strategies seem to be undermining brand equity, if consumers still see value in the premium/luxury brands and if these brands can manage to not sell on Amazon's platform, Amazon will be at a disadvantage in this quadrant. It will not be offering fair value in what consumers believe is luxury or high-quality branded product. Therefore, Amazon is potentially vulnerable here, suggesting this is a viable way for retailers to compete against Amazon—as will be discussed in subsequent chapters, which describe luxury brands' and digitally native brands' strategies.

Given this potential vulnerability, Amazon is building out a fashion platform and continues to try and entice the best brands to sell there. Fashion-loving customers coming to Amazon will be directed to a fashion platform that only the wholesale vendors have access to (not the resellers or third-party sellers). The brands that sell on this platform have better control of their brand identity and online presence, while third-party sellers are relegated to regular results pages where customers have to search through hundreds of pages of results, unlike these fashion pages where specific brands can be easily accessed.

With these new strategies, Amazon has won over fashion brands including Calvin Klein, Tommy Hilfiger, and Michael Kors. But many other higher-end luxury brands continue to hold out.

Amazon is nevertheless aggressively pursuing fashion and developed two new products in 2017: Prime Wardrobe and Echo Look. Prime Wardrobe is a platform that offers more than 1 million fashion items; it is a subscription service. Customers can order the clothing to try on for free and they are only charged for the items they keep; the rest can be returned. Echo Look is a voice-activated personal assistant that stores photographs of the customers' outfits and offers brand recommendations.

Still in Process: What Will Amazon Do in Grocery? In Healthcare?

With the purchase of Whole Foods and other food stores, Amazon is clearly going to be a player in the grocery business. There are indications that Amazon is planning to move into the pharmacy market as well, where the speculation is it will enter the specialty drug market (competitors here include CVS, Walgreens, and Express Scripts). Amazon may also investigate health-tech opportunities like telemedicine or electronic medical records. This is currently a very splintered space, but if Amazon could put together a platform that would attract all of these different apps into one place, the result would be powerful. Amazon may not be health experts, but it is customer-centric and this perspective is currently lacking in that arena.

Another indication that Amazon will move into the healthcare industry is its 2017 purchase of the biotech startup GRAIL, whose mission is to detect cancer early, when it can still be cured. GRAIL combines leading-edge computer science, high-intensity sequencing, and large-population-scale clinical studies to enhance understanding of cancer biology with the ultimate goal of developing a blood test for early-stage cancer detection. This type of business requires intensive computing power and might fit into the existing AWS business.

Finally, perhaps the strongest indication that Amazon is interested in disrupting the healthcare industry is its announcement that it would partner with Berkshire Hathaway and JPMorgan Chase in an effort to put their collective resources together to control the rise in health costs and to enhance patient satisfaction and outcomes. Although the announcement lacked specificity, experts predicted at the very least that the companies would likely be funding their own health insurance for their employees and will use this opportunity to test new models for payment and care delivery. They may also look into the healthcare distribution channel, where three companies, AmerisourceBergen, McKesson, and Cardinal Health account for the majority of revenues. There may also be opportunities in the pharmacy channel.

Preparing to Compete in the Experiential Offline World as Well

We see our customers as invited guests to a party, and we are the hosts. It's our job every day to make every important aspect of the customer experience a little bit better.

—Jeff Bezos

Finally, in the Experiential quadrant, Amazon has been mostly absent, having started as an online retailer and prioritizing technology over physical store experience. Even though there has been incredible growth in e-commerce sales, most industry experts believe there were will always be a role for the brick-and-mortar store. So, although much further behind other more traditional retailers in this quadrant, Amazon has been experimenting with different store formats. In addition, it recently purchased Whole Foods and partnered with Kohl's for product returns, and there remain constant rumors of similar new partnerships.

In implementing its physical store strategies, Amazon seems to be less focused on providing superlative pleasurable positive experiential store experiences and more focused on adding a physical presence to its frictionless shopping experience. By building and acquiring physical stores, Amazon acknowledges that brick and mortar still holds value for many customers who want to "touch and feel" the product, want goods immediately, or want to interact in a social environment. However, the Amazon priority is to find innovative ways to integrate the online/offline experience into one seamless whole.

Amazon's Own Stores

Amazon has built several branded bookstores that sell books with high customer ratings and showcase the company's growing family of gadgets. On the surface these outlets look pretty much like regular mall bookstores, but there is an important difference: When one shops in an Amazon bookstore, one has to access the Amazon app. None of the books in the store have prices shown; to learn the price, or to see reviews, consumers have to log in to its app while in the store and hold their phone up to the book or to the UPC code. This allows Amazon to connect online behavior with behavior in the store, to offer more information about the books, to charge different prices to Prime and non-Prime customers, and to continue to collect customer data that will be proactively used to better serve other customers.

In addition to the bookstores, Amazon is opening a number of small grocery or convenience stores called Amazon Go, which again teach consumers to shop with their phones using the Amazon app. Amazon Go stores use mobile e-commerce and RFID tech, machine learning, and computer vision to allow its customers to shop without having to stand in line while waiting for a cashier. In these stores, consumers swipe into the store using their phone, and their purchases are conveniently recorded by sensors and cameras that transmit information to an online processing system about the customers' movements and actions, and also about which products are ultimately chosen. When customers leave the store, charges for the purchases are automatically charged to the customers' Amazon Prime accounts.

Once this technology is thoroughly developed it is likely that Amazon will offer it to other physical retailers for a fee. If Amazon is as successful in changing customers' expectations in physical retail as it has been in online retailing, the smaller and/or less sophisticated retailers will feel market pressure to adopt the technology. Not only will this offer another source of profit for Amazon, but another source of data as well.

In addition to its Amazon Go stores, Amazon is developing another grocery concept where customers can load up a digital cart online with groceries, pay online, and then schedule a physical pickup within a two-hour window. Customers can either pick up the groceries in their own cars through curbside delivery or go into the retail store and pick them up there. There has been evidence that if customers can be incentivized to go into the store to pick up the groceries there may be opportunities for additional sales. These stores (and other retailers Amazon might purchase in the future) allow Amazon to provide a space for its online customers who still want to touch and feel the product before they buy. There seems to be some evidence that this is still desirable when it comes to apparel, grocery, furniture, and appliances.

Amazon's Purchase of Whole Foods

With the purchase of Whole Foods, Amazon has taken control of urban real estate and grocery outlets, which can double as Amazon warehouses and help Amazon more conveniently deliver to the last mile. These 450 stores are in upper-income, prime location areas that can also serve as distribution nodes for everything that Amazon sells. Speculation is that these stores will be installed with Amazon's technology, as described.

Morgan Stanley estimates that 80% of US-based Amazon Prime members, or about 38 million consumers, did not shop at Whole Foods when the acquisition was made. Further, 5 million US households, or 38% of Whole Foods shoppers at the time of acquisition, were not Prime members. Amazon's strategy appears to be to shed the high-price image that Whole Foods has historically had, and early indications suggest that the strategy is a good one.

When the Amazon-directed price drops were first announced on some items in the store, traffic at Whole Foods increased 25%. However, Amazon has yet to leverage the full potential of the acquisition. Predictions are that in the future Amazon will offer special deals to Prime members on Whole Foods products or have members-only events such as cooking classes or tastings.

Another way that Amazon will be able to lower prices at Whole Foods will be to bring its expertise to the grocer's warehouses and distribution centers. Some experts speculate that Amazon may build a network of automated warehouses that will be specifically designed for the grocery business. These facilities, like Amazon's own smart warehouses, will likely use robots and automation to lower labor costs. Additionally, Amazon can lower prices by developing its own private-label brands and has already expanded into perishable food products.

It is hard to predict exactly what effect this potential lowering of prices will have on big brands in the grocery business. Observing what has happened in other categories, however, if Amazon can become the convenient grocery shopping experience that it has become in many other categories, it seems likely that its strategies of always looking for ways to lower prices will definitely squeeze margins on the big-branded consumer packaged goods industry. Whether the brands can survive will depend upon the strength and loyalty customers have for their brand name.

Pop-Up Store Experiments

If Amazon continues to be serious about having a real presence in the apparel and fashion business, physical stores will be important here too, and already Amazon is experimenting. During the 2017 holiday season, Amazon Fashion announced limited-time pop-up stores in New York City and Los Angeles in partnership with Calvin Klein, as well as an online store on Amazon.com called "My Calvins." The pop-up stores featured celebrities and models and hosted special events.

In these pop-up stores, products can be bought immediately and taken home or delivered. The fitting rooms will feature Amazon Echo devices so that shoppers can get comfortable asking Alexa questions about fashion. The customer can also control the ambience (the lighting and music) in the fitting room simply by asking Alexa.

Conclusion

As Figure 2.1 makes clear, Amazon is the undisputed leader in the Frictionless quadrant and is continually innovating to hold this position far into the future. Its mantra is "they who control the data control the world," and Prime serves as the "flywheel" to make this happen. Using its clout, it has pushed retail prices lower and lower, giving it the leadership position in the Low Price quadrant as well.

Currently in the Product Brand quadrant Amazon offers the largest assortments, but is not quite at fair value on branded, prestigious products. Its strategy here seems to be twofold: first, to do what they can to mitigate other brands' advantages; and second, to follow up with a branded platform of its own. Finally, in the

Experiential quadrant, Amazon has acknowledged the continued importance of physical stores. Its strategy here though is to build customer experience based on frictionless shopping rather than high-end luxurious experiential interaction.

To see evidence that Jeff Bezos planned this strategy from the start, search online for the term "Amazon's Virtuous Cycle." You will see a graphic that Jeff Bezos is reported to have drawn on a napkin when he started the business in the late 1990s. This graphic suggests that growth will come as a result of "customer experience," which will drive traffic to the site, which in turn will attract sellers to the site, which in turn will provide a very large selection of products, which will lead right back to a better customer experience. Then once that cycle is complete, Amazon can leverage that advantage to lower its cost structure and thus continue to lower prices, which again will lead back to a better customer experience.

Chapter 3

Lead on Price: Everyday Low Pricing

In This Chapter: Kahn Retailing Success Strategy
- Key Leadership Strength: "Always Low Prices"
- Secondary Leadership Strength: Building an Omnichannel Experience (Frictionless)
- Fair Value in Branded Product and Experiential

Walmart was founded by Sam Walton in 1962 with the motto "Always low prices" (later changed to "Save money. Live better."). Walmart stocked a wide range of products, stayed open longer than its competition, and guaranteed the lowest prices. Although margins were low, it sold large quantities—and made big profits.

When a Walmart store came into a region, other competitors frequently suffered. Historically, its model of "operational excellence" made it the world's most streamlined distributor of goods. It replaced the "high-low" pricing strategies of many grocery stores with an "everyday low pricing" (EDLP) strategy that helped it manage inventory much more efficiently and keep costs down.

As Walmart's sales grew, its power grew, and this dynamic changed how the companies in its supply chain did business with it. This in turn gave Walmart further advantages. Walmart became so important in consumer goods that firms like Procter & Gamble built offices near Bentonville, Arkansas, Walmart's headquarters. When Walmart set goals, manufacturers found ways to meet them. For example, Walmart could convince its product manufacturers to change the size of its packaging or guarantee the lowest prices in any region for any good it sold simply because it had the power to make these demands from its suppliers.

The Strategic Advantages of an EDLP Strategy

Why did this lowest price strategy work so well? There are three reasons. First, there will always be some consumers who value a "good deal." Second, there are people who are genuinely price sensitive and are living within a budget, and for these shoppers price is the most important criterion for choosing a retailer. Finally, there are people who believe, like Jeff Bezos does, that brands are overpriced and that most products are basically commodities. So why pay more?

Following this strategy, Walmart grew so big that today it is estimated that 90% of Americans live within 10 miles of one of its stores. The *Economist* estimated that nearly four out of five Americans shopped at Walmart in 2012, meaning that its customers outnumbered the number of voters in that year's American presidential election by almost two to one.

Even with Amazon in the mix, Walmart is still the largest offline retailer in the United States and the second largest online retailer after Amazon. With $362 billion in sales in 2016, Walmart is three times bigger than the number two player, Kroger.

Walmart's leadership strategy continues to be one of low prices. But having the lowest price is no longer enough. Amazon is growing fast and competing in Walmart's playground by offering its own very low prices. Further, as shown in chapter 2, Amazon's own leadership value is in the Frictionless quadrant. For many consumers, online shopping with easy home delivery options is much more convenient than having to drive to a big-box retailer to shop.

In addition to Amazon, there are also other low-price retailers who can threaten Walmart's position. Target, although significantly smaller than Amazon and Walmart, is fighting back. And Aldi, a

German discounter that can offer very low prices typically by selling mostly private-label goods, has also become a relevant competitor in grocery. Finally, there are the dollar stores such as Dollar General that continue to invest in brick-and-mortar retail.

How Can Walmart Compete?

Walmart has to change its strategy, as relying only on low prices as its advantage is no longer sufficient in this highly competitive world. It must find another leadership value and increase its offerings in the other two quadrants as its competition ramps up customers' fair-value expectations.

One sustainable differential advantage that Walmart continues to have, however, is its large number of stores and its highly efficient operations and logistics. This gives it a competitive edge over purely online merchants because those store locations offer the opportunity for quick last-minute delivery or in-store pickup. Walmart is also expert at the complexities of handling perishable items.

Its other clear advantage is the sheer numbers of sales associates; it is the largest private employer in the United States. Recently, understanding the importance of this asset, the company has been investing more in its employees, raising salary levels, improving working conditions, and reorganizing its workforce to better fit the needs of the modern-day customer.

As competition revs up, Walmart's weaknesses in the other three quadrants outside of price has become more apparent. Its e-commerce site was significantly less effective than Amazon's; its product assortment never had fashion or premium-brand cachet; and its store experiences were not exciting enough to motivate people to visit if a more convenient online alternative was available.

Walmart's Bold New Strategy

To counter these weaknesses, Walmart purchased Jet.com for $3.3 billion in August 2016 with the dual aims of positioning the company for faster e-commerce growth and creating a seamless omnichannel shopping experience. Jet.com was chosen because it was one of the fastest-growing and most innovative e-commerce companies in the United States, cofounded by the forward-thinking Marc Lore, who previously cofounded Quidsi, the parent company of e-commerce sites Diapers.com, Soap.com, and Wag.com. As part of the deal, Lore was enlisted to run Walmart.com as president and CEO.

The purchase and integration of Jet.com also brought with it a more upscale and millennial audience that would be complementary to Walmart's core older base. Jet had also demonstrated an ability to scale quickly, had best-in-class technology, and had already attracted more than 2,400 retailers and brand partners to its platform.

Although Jet.com had originally started out with a subscription service revenue model, the company quickly pivoted to offer value through a creative lower-cost proposition. Its model gives customers the ability to drive down their final purchase costs by actively choosing less costly delivery and fulfillment options.

For example, Jet's "smart cart" allows consumers to waive their "return" options or choose to buy two items located at the same distribution center that could fit in just one box rather than choose two items at different distribution centers that could not be shipped in a single shot. If consumers choose these lower-cost delivery options, they get further discounts on their goods, which were already sold at low prices.

This "smart cart" idea now extends to Walmart.com as well. But Walmart is also leveraging its physical store advantages as part of this deal. For example, Walmart is offering lower prices to consumers who are willing to order online but pick up in the store. Essentially, with this option, consumers bear the costs of the "last mile delivery" (which is often the most expensive part of the overall delivery costs), and in return, share in those savings. By the end of fiscal year 2018 Walmart will have 1,100 curbside pickup locations and will add an additional 1,000 locations in 2019.

Building an Omnichannel Experience

This integration of Jet.com builds on Walmart's historic low-price leadership model but also helps it gain real advantages in the Frictionless quadrant, allowing the retailer to offer an omnichannel experience. Reflecting this radical change in strategy, Walmart announced on February 1, 2017, that it would be changing its name from Wal-Mart Stores, Inc. to Walmart Inc.

The strategy seems to be working. In the first year under Lore's leadership, Walmart's e-commerce sales rose 63%, with a 60% rise in digital gross merchandise volume. Its same-store sales increased 1.4% and traffic to those stores rose 1.5%.

The Walmart strategy under Marc Lore is more complicated than just building a more effective e-commerce site, however, and it maps nicely on the Kahn Retailing Success Matrix.

Plotting Walmart's Future Strategy on the Kahn Retailing Success Matrix

Personal conversations and media interviews with Marc Lore suggest that Walmart.com and Jet.com are planning improvements in all four quadrants in order to compete against Amazon. First, Walmart will continue to aim to be the lowest-price retailer. At least initially, Jet.com will remain separate and will cater to a more urban, younger, "hipper," and less price-sensitive segment.

In the Frictionless quadrant, Walmart will use the "buy online, pick up in the store" and home delivery strategies to move toward fair value. Although Walmart cannot yet compete with Amazon's last-minute delivery abilities, it can, in the short term, leverage its stores and sales associates to come pretty close to parity. In addition to the pick up in the store option, Walmart can deliver food within 10 miles from a store to 90% of the population, faster and cheaper than anyone else.

One method it is using to do this is to leverage its 1.2 million sales associates to help with delivery. Using algorithms, efficient

Figure 3.1. Plotting Walmart on the Kahn Retailing Success Matrix

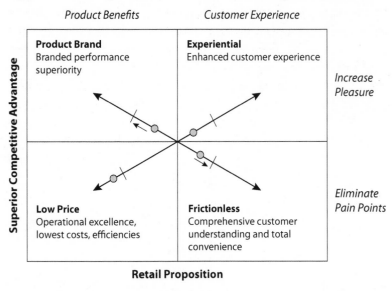

routes will be developed so that sales associates can deliver products to customers on their way home from work. This makes the cost of delivery much cheaper. Walmart is also partnering with Uber to provide a grocery delivery service from its stores. This allows Walmart to offer its shoppers the convenience that Amazon is promising.

Once it catches up in this Frictionless quadrant, Walmart will continue to invest in innovations to maintain convenient shopping options even as Amazon's innovations continue to elevate customers' expectations of what it means to offer frictionless shopping. In the Product Brand quadrant, there are plans for strategic acquisitions and development of private brands that will move Walmart to fair value or possibly above. Finally, in the Experiential quadrant Walmart is currently below expectations but has strategies in place to move to fair value here too.

These strategies are plotted in Figure 3.1. In addition to the straightforward plotting of Walmart's strengths in the Low Price and weaknesses in the Experiential quadrants, I've added arrows in the other two quadrants to represent the strategies already announced that are in process (but not completely implemented yet) to meet or exceed expectations. Hence, I have plotted Walmart currently below expectations in the Product Brand and Frictionless quadrants because even as it is rapidly investing in these quadrants, the expectations are continuing to grow because of fierce competition in the Product Brand quadrant by the vertical and luxury brands continually trying to build their own brand equities (see chapters 4 and 5) and, of course, by Amazon in the Frictionless quadrant. If Walmart and Jet's strategies pan out, Walmart can eventually meet or exceed expectations here, although exceeding them is more likely in the Frictionless quadrant than in the Product Brand quadrant.

Investing for the Future in the Frictionless Quadrant

Walmart is making a lot of investments in technology in order to compete with Amazon. One initiative is its investment in an incubator called Store No. 8, where the goal is to nurture startup businesses and help shape the retailer's future. Store No. 8 tests everything from robotics to grocery delivery.

Virtual Reality

A priority for Store No. 8 is experimenting with virtual reality, a technology that Walmart believes can help transform retail. If mobile phones have transformed the shopping experience, for example, imagine what could be possible with a 3D environment that is not as limiting as a tiny phone screen. One virtual reality experience that has been demonstrated in various media events involves allowing users who don the headsets to peer into the ocean to learn about various types of fish. Customers can wave over fish and check out the kind of equipment they may want to buy in order to catch that fish. There are other scenarios that place the user on board a virtual boat. In general, the idea with virtual reality is to situate the user in the appropriate environment or context to compel them to try out expensive products.

Internet of Things

Walmart is also investing in the connected home platform and voice technology. In August 2017 it partnered with Google to offer its customers the ability to order hundreds of thousands of products by voice. Although other retailers such as Target, Costco, and Ulta work with Google to sell its products through Google Express, only Walmart will be allowed access to the voice-enabled network. Walmart shoppers can link their Walmart accounts to Google Express and can then order the products they want, either through voice or on Google Home, or by shopping on Google Express. Their past purchase histories will be accessible to facilitate the process.

Faster, Better Delivery Options

Walmart has acquired a number of delivery and logistics startups to compete with Amazon in same-day delivery. Among them is Brooklyn-based Parcel, which has a database of every New York City building it has ever delivered to, as well as photos and detailed information about where the service entrances and elevators are in each building. Walmart has also struck a deal with the smart-access provider Latch to make deliveries easier for customers in urban areas who do not have a doorperson. Latch has hardware and software systems that allow entry into a home through methods such as using a passcode, smartphone, or smart card. Setting up temporary passcodes will allow delivery people keyless access.

Code Eight is a subsidiary of Walmart that has been testing a personal shopping service for "NYC moms." The service provides recommendations and allows users to make purchases through text messaging. Household items are delivered free within 24 hours and other purchases will arrive within two business days. Returns are picked up for free at users' homes.

Global Expansion

Walmart has also formed a strategic partnership with JD.com, China's largest e-commerce company. The two companies will integrate their platforms, supply chains, inventory management systems, and customer resources. This will enable Walmart to offer Chinese shoppers faster and more convenient access to its products. Once an order is placed, systems will determine whether a JD warehouse or a Walmart store is closer and will use the closer one as the delivery site. JD.com will also establish pickup stations at Walmart stores for those who want to shop online and pick up in the stores.

Growth in Product Brand

To build in the Product Brand quadrant, Marc Lore has announced a two-pronged acquisition strategy with the following goals: (1) to capture the "long tail" and build larger online product assortments (which can be virtually limitless in size) to provide Walmart the opportunity of serving a more diverse set of customer preferences; and (2) to differentiate by offering more premium-branded options.

Building Bigger Assortments

To fulfill the "long tail" goal and increase the size of its online product assortment, several acquisitions have been made. First, while still at Jet.com, Lore purchased home goods e-commerce company Hayneedle for $90 million in February 2016. After coming on board with Walmart, he continued acquiring e-commerce retailers, including online footwear, clothing, and accessories retailer ShoeBuy ($70 million), and outdoor gear and activewear retailer Moosejaw ($51 million).

Walmart also adds to its assortment through its own private-label brands. The company has historically had three of the top-selling private-label brands in its stores: Equate, Great Value, and Sam's Choice. Jet.com has recently announced it will launch its own brand of more premium private-label brands called "Uniquely J" that will help augment Jet's assortment and improve margins. The line currently includes 50 SKUs in the coffee, cleaning, laundry, pantry, paper, and food storage categories, and more categories are planned for the future.

Adding Prestige Brands

To add more prestige brands to its Jet.com portfolio, Lore is looking toward acquiring the "hip" digitally native vertical brands that appeal to different demographic groups than those who typically shop at Walmart.

Purchasing online retailers with strong brand cachet allows Lore to create brands much more quickly than could be done in the physical world. The plans currently are to allow these new acquisitions to operate the way they have been rather than pulling them into a typical Walmart experience. To achieve this goal, Lore purchased for approximately $70 million the online fashion retailer ModCloth, which carries plus sizes and offers vintage-style fashion, and the upscale fashion retailer Bonobos for $310 million (see chapter 4 for more information about Bonobos).

On the Walmart and physical-store side, Walmart has announced that it will partner with Hudson's Bay's Lord & Taylor to offer "stores within stores" that will feature the department store's merchandise within Walmart. This move is an attempt to "up the fashion ante" of Walmart's brands—it has never really been known as a fashion retailer, always playing second fiddle to Target in this regard.

The store within store concept allows Walmart to both leverage the higher fashion cache of the Lord & Taylor retailing brand (the oldest department store in the United States), and increase the size of its assortment. The deal calls for Lord & Taylor to be the exclusive premium department store partner. Lord & Taylor products will also be available on Walmart's website.

This is not the first time Walmart has tried to up its fashion savviness. It once had a partnership with pop star Miley Cyrus and put ads in *Vogue*, but these actions were not significant enough to make a dent in Walmart's low-price, low-prestige brand strategy. The Lord & Taylor partnership could be beneficial to both chains, potentially elevating Walmart's fashion offerings and allowing Lord & Taylor—currently a regional retailer with a Northeast-focused footprint—to grow into a national retailer without having to foot the costs of building more brick and mortar.

Trying to Meet Fair Value in Experiential

Although building superb customer experiences in its own stores is not a place that Walmart will likely be a leader, the company is beginning to experiment in this quadrant to at least keep pace with its customers' rising expectations. To achieve fair value in this Experiential quadrant it will be important for both Walmart and Jet.com to retain and acquire strong talent.

Aggressive plans are in place to assure this happens. For example, Lore has strategies in place to recruit top talent from leading universities to be product category specialists, which will include managing all categories, including online and in-store experiences. According to Lore, one of Amazon's weaknesses is that they try to solve everything with computers—and, by extension, they lose the connection to the human customer.

As acquisitions are made, it will be helpful to Walmart to keep strong talent on board with the new platform. This may be difficult, as frequently the startup culture is quite different than Walmart's culture. For example, in the Bonobos acquisition, Lore made sure to keep on board Andy Dunn, CEO and cofounder of Bonobos, to oversee the integration of the digital brands.

Plans are in place to let Bonobos maintain its unique DNA. Even after the acquisition, Bonobos will continue to operate independently and will build more of its physical stores, called guideshops, to offer superior customer experience (see chapter 4 for more detail). The investment in these guideshops will be measured not so much by return on in-store revenue, but rather in marketing or brand building value.

Using Technology to Elevate the Customer Experience

Walmart is experimenting with numerous tech ideas that could make both the store and online home shopping experience more experiential for its customers. For example, it is exploring 3D hologram technologies with Bonobos that could make it possible for customers to try on virtual clothing, allowing them to take 3D photos of themselves to see how they might look in clothing offered on the ModCloth website. The fashion brand Rebecca Minkoff, which has some items sold at Walmart.com, is also working with Walmart to explore the idea of an "interactive virtual store."

Walmart has also invested in virtual reality-based training for store associates. The technology comes from a startup called Strivr, which was founded in 2015 by Stanford athlete Derek Belch and Stanford professor Jeremy Bailenson, to allow athletes to watch immersive videos in order to give them a deeper understanding of their on-field performance. Walmart is using this technology to help store associates prepare for Black Friday crowds; the virtual reality technology allows the sales associates to see what an in-store stampede might look like and helps them figure out how to cope with it.

Finally, Walmart is investing in in-store technology to make shopping in the physical world easier. Walmart has given sales associates new or revised apps to help find inventory and drive sales. It is also developing a store concept that will have no checkout lines or cashiers. The technology is being developed to compete with the "no checkout lines" initiatives that are currently available in the Amazon Go stores.

Although Walmart is by far the largest retailer with a leadership strategy to offer low prices, there are other retailers who are competing fairly aggressively with this strategy. Next, I will briefly describe some of their strategies.

Other Successful Low-Price Retailers

Dollar Stores

Even as other retailers suffer in the Amazon era, dollar stores have been going strong. Dollar General is aggressively opening new stores and reports strong profits. Similarly, its rival Dollar Tree, which owns the Family Dollar chain, is also reporting growth.

Dollar stores are smaller in footprint than mass discounters or supermarkets. They target lower-income shoppers and focus on markets that are not necessarily well served by other retail giants. Dollar General, for example, is looking to open stores in rural and exurban locations that are located miles away from the nearest Walmart or other major retailers.

While in the past their merchandising has been somewhat of a mashup, the product assortments at these stores have been tightened up and focused more on groceries, household goods, and other consumables. While other retailers are looking to digital, these retailers are building new stores, as brick and mortar is central to their strategy.

Dollar stores are also benefiting from the Amazon effect. Currently, only about 70% of dollar store customers have smartphones, which means the demographic of a typical dollar store shopper doesn't have significant overlap with online shoppers. Further, many of the transactions in a dollar store are made in cash, which is not possible in online shopping.

In addition to people who don't or can't shop online, there is evidence that millennials who earn more than $100,000 are also shopping at dollar stores. One study shows that about 29% of the millennial dollar store customers earn over $100,000 annually—and account for about 25% of sales at those stores.

Target

Target is another important retailer competing in the Low Price quadrant and is a direct competitor to Walmart. Like Walmart, Target has historically depended on its big-box stores to drive revenues. But given the changing shopping environment, it has been growing its online business, and had a 32% year-over-year increase in online sales in 2017.

Target too is building an omnichannel strategy, encouraging its customers to order online and pick up in its stores. Plans are in place to add curbside service for pickup of online orders and to add Saturday delivery. Target is improving its supply chain and logistics capabilities by modernizing its supply chain and making strategic acquisitions such as that of Grand Junction, a transportation technology company in New York City.

Though Target had in years past capitalized on a relatively high "design" merchandising mystique within its price points, earning itself the name "Tar-zhay" ("target" pronounced as if it were a French word), recently this reputation has been tarnished as more and more of its customers have relied on the superior convenience of Amazon.

Target is responding by introducing new private brands such as the children's focused Cat & Jack, which had a very successful first-year launch. It is also looking to launch 12 new brands in infant (Cloud Island), maternity (Isabel Maternity), women's (A New Day), men's (Goodfellow & Co.), home (Project 62), and women's athletic fashion (JoyLab).

In addition, Target is investing in new fresh merchandising that is changed monthly. Customers have responded. Target announced that its comparable sales rose 3.4% in November and December 2017, well beyond Wall Street's expectations, and Target expects its sales growth to continue in the following year. Most importantly, it announced it was getting more customers into its stores.

Target is also prioritizing its small-format stores, which are aimed at three types of markets: urban centers, suburban centers, and college campuses. These stores have focused on merchandise specifically for these types of customers and can also serve as fulfillment centers for online orders.

Target has announced some partnerships with digitally native vertical brands (see chapter 4) to cater to millennial customers, although its strategy is very different from Walmart's. Target has partnered with Casper and the men's grooming subscription service Harry's, which will help the company compete against Amazon and Walmart. This partnering strategy is consistent with Target's history. In the past Target has developed its fashion brand cachet by partnering with premium luxury brands and trendy designers like Michael Graves, Missoni, Proenza Schouler, and Isaac Mizrahi, among many others.

Aldi

Aldi is a German chain grocery store that is now competing in the United States and sells privately branded knockoffs of established American foods. Aldi was founded by the Albrecht brothers, who worked in their mother's German retail business. They introduced the name "Aldi" in 1961 as a shortened version of Albrecht Diskont (Albrecht Discount). Aldi focuses on the bargain hunter.

Unlike traditional grocery stores, there are no counter service departments; everything is self-service and packaged. Customers bag their own groceries. The stores are small and they don't carry everything a more traditional grocery store might. Carts must be paid for by deposit and returned by the shopper to eliminate staffing requirements. There is no advertising.

The only staff in Aldi stores are forklift operators bringing in new pallets, cashiers, and maybe a security agent. There are no brands other than the Aldi private brands; the motive to purchase at this store is completely based on its low prices. Its store brands look like the US national brands, but they are not. The purchase process is very simple—there are no pricing trade-offs, there are no coupons, there are no sales. Estimates are that Aldi's assortments of goods will retail for 17% to 21% less than Walmart.

Aldi is so far a small player and accounts for only 1.5% of the US grocery market, but it was growing at 15% in 2017. Plans are in place to remodel older stores and to open 400 new locations as well. The company has signaled that low prices will be its singular advantage; if rivals compete on price, Aldi will respond.

Conclusion

Given the appeal of low-price strategies, the competition in this quadrant is fierce. Walmart is of course the biggest player here and has the most to lose, but it is aggressively fighting back to preserve its position. As Amazon opens more physical stores and leverages its acquisition of Whole Foods more completely, competition here is likely to heat up even further. Other low-price retailers like the dollar stores, Aldi, and Target are also aggressively protecting their market share.

Although low prices are appealing to large segments of customers, if these retailers do not respond to changing customers' expectations in the other quadrants, particularly in the Frictionless quadrant, they may lose out eventually to Amazon, which is making online shopping the norm and can ruthlessly match prices if they want and offer far superior service and convenience.

Chapter 4

Differentiate on Brand: The Vertically Integrated Brand

In This Chapter: Kahn Retailing Success Strategy
- Key Leadership Strength: Product Branding
- Secondary Leadership Strength: Lower Prices
- Fair Value in Frictionless and Experiential

As Walmart and Amazon compete in the Frictionless and Low Price quadrants, there is opportunity to capitalize on their relative weaknesses in the Product Brand and Experiential quadrants.

People have been predicting the death of brands forever. In the recession of the early 1990s magazine covers were full of such declarations. A few years later, as Amazon was introducing e-commerce to the masses, people again proclaimed that the internet and the ease in which people could compare prices would kill brands.

In the recession of 2008, pundits were saying people could no longer afford premium-priced products, and that this new price sensitivity would linger well after the economic conditions improved. But brands have been surprisingly resilient. Over and over again, evidence confirms that branded products exceed growth of the GDP by over 30%.

In this chapter I focus on a special kind of brand: vertically integrated brands (V-brands), or product brands that sell directly to the end user and typically do not partner with other retailers. They also typically do not sell branded products other than their own (although, again, they can and do in special circumstances). In essence, though, the idea is that the brand name of the product and the brand name of the retailer are one and the same.

Vertical integration is necessary for this definition, but not sufficient for market leadership. The particularly powerful V-brands that I focus on here have two characteristics that lead to market leadership. First, the brand itself must offer an emotionally compelling proposition; it must have a unique brand narrative that speaks passionately to a core customer segment. Typically, these are brand names that resonate high quality *and* high design.

Second, these V-brands reinforce that customer commitment by leveraging the advantage gained by eliminating the middleman to offer a much better price value proposition and much closer customer connection. The value pricing proposition is communicated not as a component of the brand (e.g., how "Walmart" means low prices), but as a function of creativity in the distribution system. With respect to the Kahn Retailing Success Matrix, this means they are leaders in the Product Brand quadrant, and they leverage that advantage to be leaders in the Low Price quadrant as well. They offer premium products for a great price.

V-Brands Exist in Physical Stores and Online

There are two groups of successful retailers that use a vertically integrated brand strategy to compete. First, there are vertical retail pioneers who have built powerful brands selling in physical stores. I will use as examples two V-brand retailers who are to date successfully competing against Amazon in apparel and grocery: Zara, a retailer that invented "fast fashion" and continues to delight its core segment, and Trader Joe's, a quirky grocery retailer that people "f*@%ing love," according to Colorado food writer Jenn Wohletz. Both retailers have passionate followers, and both use the fact that they sell directly to the end user to offer amazing price advantages.

Second, there are a group of relatively new V-brands that began as e-commerce retailers and have similarly cultivated a passionate group of followers. These retailers have been dubbed "digitally native vertical brands" (DNVBs) by Andy Dunn, Bonobos founder and currently senior vice president, digital consumer brands, at Walmart eCommerce. The examples I will talk about are Warby Parker, Bonobos, and Casper—each of which have reportedly passed the $100 million mark in annual revenues.

Like other e-commerce brands, DNVBs start online and market directly to the end user, hence the name: They are both digital (online) and vertical (sell directly to the end user). But DNVBs differ on the "brand" dimension. Specifically, as a group these brands are, as Dunn explains, "maniacally focused on the customer experience"; they capture every transaction and interaction and commit to understanding and delivering real value to the customer.

Because of this customer-brand focus their product gross margins are at least double that of straight e-commerce retailers (e.g., 65% vs. 30%), according to Dunn, and the contribution margins can be four to five times higher (e.g., 40% to 50% vs. 10%). Although these brands start online, the stronger ones typically extend to brick-and-mortar stores, which are extensions of their online presence and similarly very tightly controlled.

Plotting This Strategy on the Kahn Retailing Success Matrix

Since these strategies depend upon clearly differentiated branding strategies, each retailer has a unique story to tell, which I will discuss later. Even though there are these individual differences, the strategies of all the V-brand retailers have commonalties that can be mapped on the Kahn Retailing Success Matrix (see Figure 4.1).

The critical advantage for both the legacy group and DNVBs begins with their strong product brand equity. They both build on their direct-distribution strategy to become leaders in the Low Price quadrant. Then, they build on these two leadership advantages to become market leaders in the Experiential quadrant. The two groups

Figure 4.1. Plotting Vertical Brands on the Kahn Retailing Success Matrix

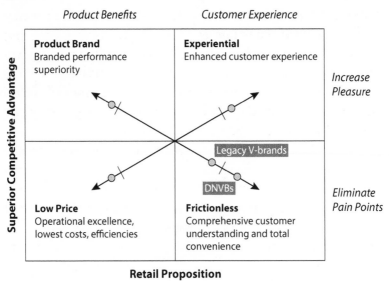

of V-brand retailers differ significantly in two ways. First, the legacy V-brand retailers are playing catch-up in the Frictionless quadrant. They have been leaders in the physical retailing world and they are slower to respond to the changing shopping patterns as a function of online shopping and mobile commerce. On the other hand, DNVBs started online and then moved to physical stores, so they are already strong in the Frictionless quadrant.

The second difference between the two groups of retailers is scale. While the DNVBs that I will discuss have passed the $100 million revenue mark, many of the new startups have not yet met that mark, and most of these retailers are not yet profitable. On the other hand, the legacy retailers that I am discussing are significantly larger. Zara, for example, reported 23 billion euros in revenues for the year 2016, and net profit of 3.16 billion euros. Similarly, Trader Joe's, which is a private company, reported $13 billion in revenues for 2015.

Superior Brand Performance

The critical leadership position of these V-brands is that they offer very strong brand equity that leads to long-term brand loyalty and brand community. These brands have established a compelling brand narrative and reinforce it through clever marketing and public relations strategies. Their reputations are cemented through strong customer-created word-of-mouth and viral videos. This means they are far above fair value in the Product Brand quadrant.

These brands frequently do not advertise, but rather their message is delivered through user-generated content. This method of promotion is not only cost-effective, but it also builds trust and increases conversion through the principle of homophily—the tendency of people to have ties with people who are similar to themselves. In other words, if someone just like you recommends something, you are more likely to like it.

By controlling the entire distribution process, V-brands can significantly improve the shopping experience both by removing pain points (as a result of having extensive customer data and continual customer interaction and feedback) and providing personalized and fun experiential events and processes.

Lower Prices by Passing on Lower Costs Obtained through Elimination of Layers

There are several advantages to the direct model. First, through direct sources of supply, retailers can achieve an average reduction of between 2% and 4% in cost of goods sold by eliminating inefficiencies in the supply chain. The direct relationship with suppliers also allows for speedy iterations on product design and more rapid response to demand changes and fashion trends.

Second, by eliminating the other retailing layers in the distribution chain to the end user, V-brands can eliminate excessive margins and pass those savings on. This allows them to compete more effectively on price. It also allows them to better control their brand narrative because there is no other retailer who is communicating at the point-of-sale. Finally, it gives them total control of their customer data.

The other advantage of the direct model is better control of inventory, which helps manage the need for end-of-season price discounting. Typically, retailers using this strategy offer best price values using "everyday low pricing" strategies, and minimal to no price promotions. Thus, these brands are above fair value in the Low Price quadrant.

Exceptional Customer Experiences within Physical Stores

The two types of V-brand retailers differ in their experiential strategies as they come at it from different directions, but they both are way above fair value in offering physical store experiences that excite their customers.

The legacy retailers, such as Zara, Trader Joe's, Ikea, Victoria's Secret, and others, have always differentiated themselves through their stores. Because these retailers are direct, they are closer to their customers and they can respond to customer needs in their stores faster. As I will describe, for example, Zara's strategy is to listen intently to what customers want and to make sure those designs are in their stores as quickly as possible. Designs that don't sell are just as quickly eliminated. Trader Joe's stores, meanwhile, are unique, friendly, quirky, and again very responsive to customer tastes.

For DNVBs, the opening of their first physical stores allows for experimentation. Many of the first stores for these retailers were pop-ups, where consumer behavior could be observed before making costly investments. Also, DNVBs benefit from intimate knowledge of how consumers browse, search, and shop because of extensive data from the online shopping experience. As a result, when DNVB retailers open their first stores they look different from legacy retailers' stores.

For example, for many DNVBs the physical stores do not carry extensive inventory, but rather operate as showrooms that augment the digital experience rather than replace it. These showrooms provide opportunities for the consumer to touch and feel the product, interact with knowledgeable sales associates, and then make the final purchase online with at-home delivery.

Also, these new DNVB stores can offer experiential opportunities based on observed online behaviors. For example, Alo Yoga ("Alo" is an acronym for "Air, Land, and Ocean"), which sells athletic apparel, opened a flagship store in Beverly Hills that houses yoga and fitness studios and has a lounge area for customers to relax. When Birchbox opened its first store in New York City, it organized it by product category rather than by brand. It also provided try-on bars and areas for the customer to learn.

Although they come from different directions, both types of retailers are able to hold their own on changing customer expectations with respect to in-store experiences, so both are above fair value in the Experiential quadrant.

Frictionless Convenience

The biggest difference between the two types of V-brands is in the Frictionless quadrant. Since DNVBs started online, they can anticipate customer needs and respond similarly to the way Amazon can respond to customer needs. Further, when they build physical stores, the online and offline experiences are instantly merged, as their customers are used to engaging with them one-on-one online. Like Amazon, DNVBs have extensive customer data and can design customer-centric strategies.

The legacy players are playing catch-up in this space. Some of them are rapidly developing omnichannel strategies that offer a seamless experience online and offline. Others are lagging and their e-commerce presence is quite limited.

These strategies are plotted on the Kahn Retailing Success Matrix in Figure 4.1.

Will These Retailers Be Successful?

When plotted on the matrix, the strategies of these firms look quite strong. DNVB retailers are above fair value, market leaders in all *four* quadrants, not just the suggested two, and the legacy retailers are above fair value in three of the four. These are obviously very compelling positions. But there are risks going forward.

Success of Legacy V-Brands

For the legacy retailers, their weakness in the Frictionless quadrant can be an Achilles' heel. As Amazon gets stronger and stronger, customers' expectations in this quadrant will grow quickly and customers will likely have little patience for retailers who cannot meet their convenience and delivery requirements.

Further, although Amazon is currently behind these retailers in terms of product brand and physical store experiential environments, Amazon may seek to mitigate its weakness with strategic acquisitions. As mentioned in chapter 2, Amazon is making moves in fashion, and with the purchase of Whole Foods Amazon can compete in these quadrants in grocery if it desires. With Walmart's acquisition of Jet.com and other DNVBs, it too may be able to compete effectively.

Success of DNVB Retailers

DNVB retailers certainly have a viable strategy in place, and, so far, the math works. But these players are still quite small, and most are not profitable yet. If they can successfully scale up, they may be able to secure 30% operating margins (according to Marc Lore), which would be viable. But they have to get over the hump—which some experts estimate at the $100–$200 million revenue mark.

The more successful DNVBs (such as Warby and Casper) have a fighting chance, but many of the smaller ones may get stuck in the $50 million revenue range and not make it in the long term. Alternatively, some may be bought out by retailers with deep pockets, such as when Walmart bought out Bonobos and ModCloth, Unilever bought out Dollar Shave Club, and Amazon bought Zappos. The "Top 25 DNVBs of 2017" sidebar lists the most successful digitally native vertical brands of that year.

Further, because these DNVBs have outside funding, they do not initially have to depend on cash flow and profitability to stay viable as the legacy brands did. This outside funding has helped DNVBs grow revenues much more quickly than legacy brands such as Nike, Patagonia, or Victoria's Secret could. But eventually DNVBs will still need two to three times their acquisition costs in margin to succeed.

Even if they can grow their revenues, the other problem with many of these new DNVBs is that they are often fashion brands. Many of them are banking on the tastes of millennials and Generation Z, and those tastes can be fickle. As retail commentator Richie Siegel suggested on The Business of Fashion website, "If Ralph Lauren is not successful is it because of its model, or because the aesthetic has ceased to make sense to Gen Z'ers who shun grandpa's ties and blazers?"

Top 25 DNVBs of 2017

- Alo Yoga
- Away Travel
- Birchbox
- Bonobos
- Casper
- Draper James
- Eloquii
- Everlane
- Glossier
- Harry's
- Kopari
- M.Gemi
- MM.LaFleur
- Morphe
- MVMT
- Outdoor Voices
- Parachute
- Perverse
- Quay Australia
- Rockets of Awesome
- Rothy's
- Saxx Underwear Co.
- Stance
- Thirdlove
- Warby Parker

Source: Pixlee, *The Top 25 Digitally Native Vertical Brands Report*, 2017.

How Did These Retailers Build Their Brand Narratives? Some Examples

The key to these V-brand retailers' success is their brand story, and each is unique. I will summarize the marketing strategies of a few of the key retailers.

Zara

Zara, an international clothing retailer owned by Inditex and headquartered in Spain, was founded in 1975. From the start, its mission was to provide clothing that offers fashionable new designs (many times copies of popular, higher-priced fashion styles) that were made from quality materials—and were affordable. To deliver on this mission, the company invested in a manufacturing and distribution process that could reduce lead times and react to trends faster. It invested in IT extensively and expanded globally. There are now over 7,000 Zara stores, and the retailer is still growing rapidly.

Zara was one of the originators of "fast fashion." Unlike the 12-to-18-month lead times of many of its fashion competitors, Zara could design and sell its collection in only four weeks. Most fashion brands are top-down, depending upon well-known, talented designers to dictate the styles and fashions for the season. Zara works from the bottom up. The retailer watches trends and consumers' reactions to them, sees what people are wearing, monitors fashion blogs and fashion shows, and then produces designs that it believes will appeal to its customers.

This approach largely works well, although occasionally there are bumps in the road, primarily around accusations of putative plagiarism. The company has been sued in the past by indie designers and high-end brands, but most of the cases get resolved in Zara's favor because the company is able to tweak the design enough to get around copyright laws. This approach may not serve designers well, but customers react very positively.

Being so customer-focused means that Zara is less likely to guess wrong on which styles will be hot, and therefore less likely to have excess inventory at the end of the season. Zara also increases the desirability of its designs by producing less of each style and changing what it has on its sales floors frequently. This means that it carries much less inventory of any particular style, again lowering the risk of failed forecasting.

This frequent turnover of inventory drives the customer into the store more often to see what is new. It also teaches the customer that if she sees something she likes, she should purchase it right away because it might not be there next time. Zara's influence on the marketplace has been so great that traditional houses like Prada and Louis Vuitton have started to make four to six collections each year rather than just two.

With these strategies in place, each of the styles only stays in the store for three to four weeks, thus inventory turns 17 times per year. In order to encourage more purchasing, Zara's founder, Amancio Ortega, has encouraged his customers to think of clothing as a perishable commodity, or "disposable clothing." People should buy the latest trends, wear them, then throw them out, and buy the next trend.

Critical to Zara's brand equity is that it can forecast and produce the hottest fashion designs reliably. That it has accomplished this consistently in a notoriously fickle industry is a function of the systems and processes that are in place. It is a not a function of luck, but rather of Zara being very customer focused.

Importance of Physical Stores and Sales Associates

Central to its fashion strategy are its sales associates who are trained to listen to customers and to report back what they hear. First thing every morning, the floor staff and store managers meet to discuss the previous day's best-selling items, which items were returned, what were shoppers saying, and what trends were noticed on the floor. No detail is too small, and all customer comments are taken seriously.

These data points are entered into a system, and headquarters uses sophisticated technology to data-mine the daily updates and use them to help determine future offerings. The data is used by in-house designers to make consumer-friendly, trend-appropriate offerings. In addition to observing behavior in Zara stores, buyers visit universities, nightclubs, and other locales to see what people are wearing. Recently, they have also monitored social media, online talk, and bloggers.

Its marketing strategy is not based on advertising, but rather on word of mouth and retail displays, thus its stores are a key part of its marketing. Zara's store priority is now focused on flagship stores in very high-traffic locations, frequently next to luxury brands such as Prada and Chanel. It is closing smaller stores. The store window displays showcase the most fashionable pieces in the collection and change often.

Zara's Vertically Integrated Supply Chain

Complementing this customer-centric approach is a vertically integrated supply chain that ships new products to stores twice a week. Better inventory control eliminates the need for warehouses.

Zara also has a more sophisticated procurement and manufacturing approach. The more fashionable (and hence riskier) items are made in company-owned factories in Spain, northern Portugal, and Turkey. The items with more predictable demand patterns, such as basic T-shirts, are made with low-cost suppliers elsewhere. From its own factories in Spain, Zara transports its product by air directly to the stores around the world, eliminating layers and making delivery times much faster than retailers who manufacture their goods in Asia can accomplish. This helps ensure that Zara is first with trendy fashions and proves to be much more flexible.

Zara's Weaknesses

As mentioned, Zara is very strong in its physical stores, but unlike the DNVBs it does not have much of a digital history (it only offered online opportunities in 2010), and they are behind in mobile commerce. In 2017 experts estimated only 5.5% of sales at Inditex were online, which is surprising given its target segment is millennials and Gen Z'ers. Part of this slow movement is likely a function of Zara's dependence on the interactions in the store to drive its market intelligence.

However, Inditex has announced that it is planning full integration of brick-and-mortar stores with online shopping, and the opening of the new stores will reflect that strategy. For example, customers will be able to pick up and return online purchases in-store. The company is also prioritizing its online strategy. Online customers are directed to Zara's homepage, which showcases its rapidly changing fashion.

Zara's price leadership may also be under threat from Amazon, especially if Amazon develops any credibility on the fashion front. Zara also has other competition. There are other fast fashion retailers like H&M and Mango, which are cheaper, but whose quality may not be considered as high. There are new digital fashion aggregators like Lyst, Farfetch, Spring, Yoox, and Net-a-Porter that are credible competition as well.

Trader Joe's

Trader Joe's, which is owned by Aldi, has stated that its mission is to deliver high-quality food and beverage with a sense of warmth, friendliness, fun, individual pride, and company spirit. Like the other retailers described in this chapter, Trader Joe's eliminates layers so that it can get cost advantages and pass those along to the end users as lower prices. It buys direct from suppliers in volume, which results in better prices for goods. Further, it does not charge its suppliers slotting fees for putting items on the shelf, which further lowers the selling price.

Although Trader Joe's does sell third-party goods, there are not a lot of national branded items available in its stores. Experts estimate that 80% of Trader Joe's products are "in-house," and not available anywhere else. The retailer's website states: "At Trader Joe's, you won't find a lot of branded items. You'll find unconventional and interesting products in the Trader Joe's label as well as everyday basics. We buy products we think are winners and that'll find a following among our customers. Sometimes it's a product we intend to stock as long as it sells well; and sometimes we buy a product which is in limited supply, sell through it, and you won't find it again. It's all part of the shopping adventure at Trader Joe's." So, like Zara, Trader Joe's encourage customers to buy when they see things and to understand that certain products may not always be available.

Trader Joe's has a vibe, and is one of the few non-mega grocers that is succeeding in a retailing world of behemoths: Walmart, Amazon, Costco, and Target. No other chain offers what it does: unique, natural brands you can't get anywhere else. The Trader Joe's shopping experience continues to please customers who will often wait on long lines and deal with stock-outs without complaining, mostly due to their fierce loyalty to the quirky environment.

Trader Joe's Vulnerability

With Amazon's purchase of Whole Foods, Trader Joe's is certainly in the crosshairs. Right after the announced purchase, when Amazon cut prices at Whole Foods in a much-publicized play, 10% of all Trader Joe's customers defected to Whole Foods. That figure went down to 6% as the weeks went on, suggesting that there is strong loyalty to Trader Joe's, but what the future will bring is uncertain.

In addition, although Trader Joe's has very loyal shoppers in its physical stores, it is lagging significantly in the Frictionless quadrant. Trader Joe's does not have a notable online strategy yet. You can order Trader Joe's groceries online, yes, but they are delivered through third-party services. You can also order via Amazon. This may not currently be a big issue as grocery and food are still categories that are primarily being bought offline, but if customer behavior changes over time, Trader Joe's will be at a significant disadvantage.

Trader Joe's does not seem to be particularly invested in the online universe in general. While it has social media pages, those pages are run primarily by fans. So far, loyalty to Trader Joe's quirky stores and unique product mix has protected it against too much poaching by Amazon/Whole Foods, but time will tell here.

Warby Parker

Warby Parker is often cited as the prototypical DNVB. The company was founded in 2010 in Philadelphia, when the founders, Neil Blumenthal, Dave Gilboa, Jeff Raider, and Andy Hunt, were MBA students at Wharton.

The designer eyewear industry was a large market at the time, with over $65 billion of revenue, and was dominated by a single company, Luxottica, which had significant market share. This dominance was somewhat masked because the company operated under many different brand names. For example, Luxottica owns eyewear-only brands like Ray-Ban, Oakley, and Oliver Peoples; it has the licenses for fashion brands such as Chanel, Versace, Polo and D&G; it owns eyewear retailers, including LensCrafters, Sunglass Hut, Pearle Vision, and works with Target and Sears in their optical divisions. It also owns the vision insurance company EyeMed.

Because of Luxottica dominance, the industry had very high markups. Products whose manufacturing and distribution costs came in at $25 could be sold at $400 retail after including wholesale, licensing, and retail markups. Further, this category was sold almost exclusively in physical stores.

But the Warby Parker founders speculated that if they could convince consumers to buy online, and if they could manage their entire distribution cycle by selling directly to end users (thus eliminating many layers), they could produce a very high-quality product at a quarter the retail price.

Customer-Centric Innovations That Built the Brand

One of the big issues in selling eye glasses directly online was that consumers were used to trying on frames in physical stores. How could consumers be convinced to purchase eye glasses online without trying them on?

The team's first big innovation to solve this problem was their "Home Try-On" program where consumers could try up to five frames at home for free for five days. This program was incredibly successful right out of the gate because it was convenient, easy, eliminated any risk, and offered people high-quality glasses at an amazing price: $99. Equivalent designer prescription glasses were going for $300 and more at the time.

There were other unanticipated benefits from the Home Try-On program. It turns out people are pretty bad at determining for themselves which glasses fit their faces. So, when people received their glasses at home, they would frequently post photos of themselves on social media sporting different frames and asking friends for advice. This generated trusted public awareness of the brand. More than 50% of sales were generated through word-of-mouth referrals.

True to the DNVB mantra, the Warby founders were maniacally focused on customer service. They made their website very user-friendly, anticipating and answering any questions that a consumer may want to ask a sales associate in a physical store. Sometimes, consumers emailed questions and the founders themselves replied. All this attention to detail paid off: Warby's net promoter score was over 85, higher than Apple's and Amazon's.

In addition to the powerful word-of-mouth referrals, Warby had a good story to tell, and the New York City media were interested. One of the first publications that wrote about Warby was *GQ*, which called it "the Netflix of eyewear." The public response was so great after this exposure that Warby hit its first-year sales target in three weeks and generated a waiting list of 20,000 people. Soon, other fashion magazines and main street media were telling their story as well.

Warby continued to innovate with clever marketing and retailing strategies. For example, during New York Fashion Week, Warby had their friends and some professional models go to the New York Public Library the day before the Fashion Week events formally started. Warby then invited reporters to go to the library, and since it was a slow day, many reporters were available.

At a set time, each of the Warby representatives, who were scattered throughout the library sitting at different tables, held up a book that was covered with the Warby brand's light blue color. Each book that was held up had the name written on it of one of their eyeglass styles as the book's title (Warby's eyeglass style names are all famous literary references). Having everyone hold up these light blue books at the same time resulted in vivid visual imagery.

The coordinated action made for great photographs and the event was covered widely. Over time Warby created other provocative events and put together pop-up stores with interesting themes. It also retrofitted a school bus as an eyeglass store and drove around the country in this "bus-store" visiting campuses. All of this activity generated widespread media coverage in the *New York Times*, *Vogue*, *Esquire*, *WWD*, *Forbes*, *People*, the *Wall Street Journal*, and *Glamour*.

Adding to this compelling brand narrative was exceptional customer service fueled by engaged employees. The people who worked at Warby were also fervent believers in the brand—especially because Warby promised to donate one pair of eye glasses to someone in need for every pair it sold. The employees became loyal ambassadors of the brand.

Warby personifies everything a successful DNVB should be: an efficient distribution channel delivering a high-quality product at a reasonable price directly to the consumer. It has a valuable brand narrative and strong customer community that generates tons of social media and word of mouth to promote the brand.

Warby was also one of the first DNVBs to consider opening up stores. Based on information learned from its pop-up stores and bus trips, it opened its first physical showroom in New York City. Analyzing the data carefully after that opening, it learned that the physical stores did not cannibalize online sales, but rather increased sales overall. Opening physical stores in the right locations, with an eye for whimsy, design, and attention to the local area, became a priority. It now has over 60 stores in the United States and is still growing.

Warby is definitely a success story. It has raised $215 million and has been valued at $1.2 billion. Its latest move is to fund a $15 million optical lab in upstate New York that will help with greater quality control and faster delivery. It is also exploring ways to assess visual prescriptions via digital applications on a personal device.

Bonobos

Bonobos was launched in 2007 by Andy Dunn and Brian Spaly as an exclusively online retailer with the goal of selling men's pants that promised a great fit and style while minimizing time and hassle. Their product—with a curved waistband, a medium rise, and a tailored thigh fit designed to eliminate the "khaki diaper butt"—was much better than alternatives and soon inspired great word of mouth. The brand grew.

Bonobos expanded to include men's shirts, sweaters, and jackets. In 2012 Andy (Brian left in 2009 to run Trunk Club), recognizing the need for customers to "touch and feel" in the apparel category (especially in clothing that is marketed on fit), set up an exclusive partnership with Nordstrom to sell Bonobos product in their 100 Nordstrom stores. This was a win-win for both partners. For Bonobos, it was helpful to get scale. For Nordstrom, the DNVB brought a younger customer into the store. Nordstrom also saw it as an opportunity to improve its own digital practices.

Eventually, Bonobos opened its own physical stores that they called "guideshops." These stores were unlike normal men's retailing stores in that they were showrooms only—they had no inventory. Given they didn't have to carry full inventory, the showroom could keep items for every size and style so the customer could try anything on he wanted in the store and never have to experience stockouts. After trying on the product, he could order online and have the product delivered to his home. The stores turned out to be the best customer acquisition channel Bonobos had.

In June 2017, as mentioned earlier, Walmart purchased Bonobos for $310 million. The brand will not be sold in Walmart stores, but will be sold on Jet.com.

Casper

Casper was founded in 2013 and launched in 2014. Similar to Warby, Casper's creators recognized that the mattress industry was a large market (over a $14-billion business) dominated by two major companies: Tempur Sealy and Serta Simmons, which together controlled over 70% of bedding wholesale shipments. The industry was growing, but primarily by raising prices.

Consumer Reports reported that mattresses carried a heavy price tag because the margins in the category were higher than for any other product in a furniture store. Frequently the gross profit margins were 30% to 40% each for wholesalers and retailers. High-end luxury models could command even higher margins.

Further, the sales process was so unpleasant people couldn't wait to get out of the store. Most customers knew nothing about mattresses and were embarrassed to lie on a mattress and imagine sleeping to test it (especially with people watching). Delivery was also very slow.

Like Warby's Home Try-On program, Casper came up with a clever innovation that made the process easier and generated great social media and viral word-of-mouth publicity. It figured out how to deliver the mattresses in a box (the size of a mini fridge) on a bicycle. Customers would video themselves opening up the boxes and post the videos on Instagram. Casper also promised a risk-free experience: People could try the product for 100 nights, and if they didn't like it, Casper would pick their mattress up and take it back.

Casper also took the pain out of the decision-making process by limiting the choices that had to be made. There was only one type of mattress, which was designed as a combination of memory and latex foam. Further, Casper priced its mattress way below the prices of the other mattresses on the market.

Although there are other online-centric mattress startups, including Leesa, Yogabed, and Tuft & Needle, Casper is probably the most famous. The Casper model was so successful that it generated revenues of over $100 million in less than two years. Its brand promise? To provide the best mattress possible at an affordable price, sell a single model, and deliver it quickly for free—with a 100-day trial period.

Like other DNVBs, Casper has recently started thinking about opening physical stores. At the end of 2017 it announced that it would open 15 pop-up stores across the nation, including the markets of Atlanta, New Jersey, and New York.

Other Retailers Who Have Learned from the DNVB Playbook

DNVBs have inspired other retailers to experiment with showrooms that do not stock inventory but offer retailers a way to interact with their customers, build relationships, and collect useful data for future proactive activity and recommendations. For example, Samsung opened a store in New York City where customers can play with the company's newest devices and gadgets, learn how to use smart appliances, and experiment with virtual reality.

There is no pressure to buy—in fact, the only things that can be purchased in the store are coffee and bagels. The idea is to build customer knowledge and loyalty for the brand. The store also offers events that draw customers in—in the first year, Gwen Stefani performed, there were cooking demonstrations, and various other interactive installations. The company estimated that within the first ten months the store was open, more than a half million people visited the space.

Nordstrom has also expressed interest in trying out the showroom idea. The first "Nordstrom Local" prototype was launched in West Hollywood in 2017. This store features nail beauty services, tailoring, and style advice. It is in the same vein as Bonobos's guideshops in that it doesn't have inventory but rather allows customers to check out and try on garments, and then go online to order. The new store has dressing rooms and a bar featuring alcoholic and nonalcoholic drinks. "Nordstrom Style Boards" provide personalized fashion recommendations that can be viewed on a phone, and items can then be purchased directly from Nordstrom.com. Although there is no buyable inventory available, there are personal stylists on hand who can order the items, which can be picked up that same day at the store if the order is made before 2 p.m.

Conclusion

Many retailers who are successfully holding their own in this disruptive retailing environment are engaging in vertically integrated brand (V-brand) strategies. These retailers sell their branded product brands directly to the end user. The successful ones have a compelling brand proposition and have leveraged significant cost advantages from eliminating layers both in distribution and in the supply chain. They have passed these cost advantages on to their customers and are able to sell high-quality, premium-branded products at low prices.

There are two classes of V-brands. The first are the legacy brands who built this strategy through their physical stores. According to a 2017 Interbrand survey, some of the most valuable brands in the world fit this model: H&M, Zara, and Ikea, all of which rank in the top 25 globally. These brands are doing well even with the threat of Amazon's entry into their business. They have private brands that cannot be purchased anywhere else and they have very loyal customers. As the shopping experience shifts more to online purchasing, the challenge for these brands is to keep their dominance in the new channel and to make sure that they offer an integrated online-offline experience.

The other V-brands, termed digitally native vertical brands, started online first and have since moved into physical stores. These have passionate, loyal communities who help promote the brands through active social media engagement. Because they started in the digital world, they have amassed a great deal of data about their customers and can offer high-quality products at a low price and provide exceptional online and offline customer experiences. Their challenge is to now scale up. The most successful of these new breeds—Warby Parker, Casper, and Bonobos—have passed the $100 million revenue mark but are still far smaller than the traditional retailers. Many of them are also depending upon external funding rather than cash flow and profitability to fund their businesses.

Chapter 5

The Paradox of Luxury: When Low Prices and Accessibility Are Undesirable

In This Chapter: Kahn Retailing Success Strategy
- Key Leadership Strength: Unparalleled Luxurious Product Brand Superiority
- Secondary Leadership Strength: A Luxurious Customer Experience
- Fair Value in Frictionless When Appropriate
- Luxury Brands Control Accessibility and Stay Away from Lower-Price Strategies

In spite of the continued online emphasis on price transparency, the lure of luxury shopping endures. The luxury retail market is growing faster than any other category according to Edited, a retail analytics tech company. Similarly, Bain & Co. reported that the luxury market will reach a new normal of 4% to 5% annual growth through 2020. Indications are that Chinese middle-class consumers will once again purchase luxury. And the millennials and Generation Z (Gen Z) are starting to connect with luxury brands like their baby boomer and Generation X parents did.

With occasional blips as a result of economic downturns (like the Great Recession), political dynamics (like the Chinese government's anticorruption campaigns that cracked down on extravagant gifts and parties), or the terrorist attacks that threatened European tourism, luxury sales have been extraordinarily robust over the past decades. While it is often difficult to predict the hot luxury brand of any season, the top luxury brands in the 1950s (e.g., Gucci, Dior, Chanel, Louis Vuitton, Cartier) are still the top luxury brands today.

What Is Luxury? And How Does It Differ from Premium-Priced?

Yes, luxury brands are more expensive than "premium-priced" brands, but there are also other important differences between them. Premium-priced brands are defined by a quality/price value ratio, where higher quality will demand a higher price. But for luxury, higher quality is necessary but not sufficient. Adam Smith defined luxury brands as not only very expensive, but also limited in supply and difficult to procure.

Luxurious products and experiences are defined by unique characteristics that cannot be copied, like heritage, legacy, tradition, blood (family), celebrity, and, more recently, designers. True luxury brands are timeless icons, magical, and more like religion and art than commerce. Just as it is difficult to put a quality/price value on a Monet painting, so luxury brands have a heritage that is irreproducible. "Luxury brands are the ambassadors of local culture and refined art de vivre," writes Jean-Noël Kapferer, a European expert on luxury.

True luxury value ignores customer-centric ideas. Luxury brands and designers are the arbiters of taste and of design, not blind followers of customers' wishes. Luxury is aspirational; people desire to be among royalty. Luxury is not for the masses, not for the common people, and is not democratic.

Luxury is also about scarcity. There is only one Italy, for example, and the "Made in Italy" merchandising mark, established in 1980, celebrates that fact. A 2009 Italian law stipulated that only products *totally* made in Italy (including planning, manufacturing, and packaging) could differentiate themselves by the prestigious "Made in Italy" mark. Italy celebrates its manufacturing expertise and heritage by promoting its factories, such as the Maserati or Parmigiano Reggiano cheese factories, as tourist attractions—as theater. Other

European brands, like Louis Vuitton, a French brand, support Italian expertise by advertising that they make their shoes in Italy. Customers respond to this distinctiveness. A BCG study that asked respondents "Which country of manufacturing do you consider is the best for luxury products?" reported Italy was the leader for 29% of respondents. France was second with 23%, and all other countries were much lower.

Another "rule" of luxury is that you cannot compare luxury products to anything else. For example, champagne either comes from France's Champagne district or it is not champagne. Therefore, you cannot compare prices of other sparkling wines to French champagne; they are fundamentally different entities. Similarly, cognac is defined on an ambiguous scale—not exact age, an alignable attribute, but rather by XO ("extra old") or VSOP ("very superior old pale"). It is not about traditional marketing "positioning," where products are compared to one another to establish a competitive advantage.

Total control of the whole manufacturing and distribution chain is also a requirement for the most exclusive luxury brands. Hermès, probably the most prestigious, controls everything under its brand name and does not issue licenses. Although luxury brands may be sold at luxury retailers such as Saks, Neiman Marcus, Le Bon Marché, Galeries Lafayette, Harrods, or Selfridges, many of the luxury brands prefer to go direct to exercise more control.

All of this defines luxury, but also defines the "paradox of luxury," as these requirements would seem to stand in the way of growth. The very high-end luxury market is quite small, by definition. The only way to grow, then, is to appeal to a broader market by issuing licenses and expanding distribution channels. But if luxury brands issue too many licenses and become ubiquitous, they lose their cachet. Brands like Pierre Cardin, and even Gucci and Ralph Lauren, overlicensed and overdistributed and had to take back control because of serious brand dilution.

Pricing also has to be controlled. Thus, true luxury brands do not ever discount, even if they have excess inventory. Because of the short shelf life of seasonal brands, at these top luxury houses seasonal products are priced 20 to 30 times higher than the more timeless designs, and only a limited amount is produced. If these seasonal products do not sell in time for the next inventory shift, they may be burned rather than discounted.

The Social Signaling Role of Luxury

Luxury brands are signals that the wearer is of the elite class and has the money to purchase such exclusive designs. For the signaling to be effective, those who cannot afford luxury have to recognize the brand to appreciate it. But if the luxury becomes too familiar it loses its cachet.

Logos are often used to signal the brand, but they can be overdone. Interesting research by Han, Nunes, and Drèze showed that the desirability of logos can be described by a 2×2 matrix. One axis is defined by wealth—one either has the money to afford luxury or doesn't. The other axis is defined by the social need to signal. Some people want others to know they can afford luxury, while others are only interested in certain elites knowing. This framework produces four categories of consumers of luxury.

"Patricians" have money and only care if the elite (not the masses) appreciate their purchases. They prefer quiet signals or "griffes," special identifiers that people in the know can recognize, like the Burberry check *inside* the trench coat, or the Cartier bracelet that cannot be removed. For these people, loud logos are vulgar.

"Proletarians" also do not wear luxury logoed products, but this is because they either cannot afford them or do not care about signaling status to others. They generally do not purchase any luxury.

"Parvenues" have money and want people to know it. They want to disassociate themselves from the have-nots. Here, logos are important identifiers. Parvenues generally shun counterfeits, because they value the higher quality and heritage of the genuine luxury products.

"Poseurs" don't have the money yet but they aspire to have it. Since they cannot afford the high-end luxury brands, they are more likely to buy counterfeits. If they buy genuine luxury they can only afford the low end of an expensive brand, either a diffusion brand (Marc by Marc Jacobs or AX by Armani) or an entry-level luxury product like cosmetics or key chains. These "poseurs" can be troublesome for a luxury brand because if they indulge in too many conspicuous logos or counterfeit products, the exclusivity and prestige of the true brand is threatened.

How Will Luxury Change in the Future?

Experts predict that the millennials and Gen Z will account for 45% of the luxury market by 2025. Will this idea of exclusivity and aspirational values jive with the goals of the younger generation who purport to value transparency and authenticity?

Some studies have shown that the younger generations seem to value experiences more than material possessions, so at the very least luxury brands must provide not just superior product brands but also overall luxurious, exclusive customer experiences. The younger, digitally native generations value convenience, and expect 24/7 environments. Luxury has to think through how to make its products and experiences more accessible without losing the exclusivity.

Early indications are that Gen Z will take to luxury more than millennials because the millennials came of age in the Great Recession, whereas Gen Z arrived in flusher economic times. Gen Z'ers, although mobile savvy, have not abandoned physical stores. Some of the more interesting retail concepts have capitalized on Gen Z's proclivity for social media and physical retail by providing settings where nothing is sold but customers can come into a well-designed interactive physical environment and take photos of themselves to be posted on Instagram or Facebook.

For example, the Museum of Ice Cream in Miami Beach (also located in other top US cities like New York City and San Francisco) charges $38 per person for admission to a series of pink-painted rooms tangentially related to the history of ice cream, each of which provides crazy opportunities for selfies (like jumping into a "swimming pool" of plastic sprinkles or swinging on a banana swing). Another type of urban luxury appeals to millennial or Gen Z "hypebeasts." For this consumer, the hype is the appeal. Here the product doesn't matter, it is *just* the hype (the brand)—the logo in and of itself that has value.

Plotting This Strategy for Luxury Brands on the Kahn Retailing Success Matrix

Historically, luxury retailers have competed by providing unequaled high-quality branded products. But as I have argued throughout this book, leadership in one quadrant is not sufficient in today's very highly competitive retailing world. Most of the luxury retailers are seeking to leverage their brand cachet to produce superior luxurious customer experiences as well.

Luxury retailers also have to be mindful of ever-increasing customer expectations in the Lower Price and Frictionless quadrants. These two values are tricky because effective execution here runs counter to the principles of luxury. As mentioned earlier, the very top luxury brands make a point of pricing exorbitantly high, making it difficult for most people to purchase the product. A special edition Hermès Birkin bag can range as low as $10,000 or as high as $150,000—and they are only available to a small group of people who have the right connections. This again is the paradox of luxury: The very principles of business growth and success bump heads with its exclusivity tenets. These ideas are plotted in Figure 5.1.

Accessible luxury—typically American brands (e.g., Michael Kors and Coach)—followed the luxury strategy with branded products but pay more attention to growth objectives and aim for fair value in the Low Price and Frictionless quadrants. These luxury retailers frequently discount their products and sell in outlets. These strategies grow top-line sales but can dilute the value of the brand. This strategy for these accessible luxury retailers is plotted in Figure 5.2.

Figure 5.1. Plotting Luxury on the Kahn Retailing Success Matrix

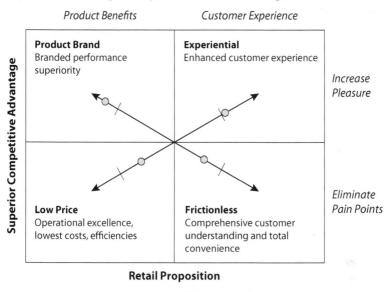

Many of these accessible luxury retailers have begun to rethink this strategy because of the long-term brand value deterioration it has caused.

In the next sections I will outline the strategies that legacy luxury retailers, accessible luxury retailers, and new e-commerce entrants are developing to compete in all four of the Kahn Retailing Success Matrix quadrants.

Primary Value: Unparalleled Luxurious Product Brand Superiority

Since the luxury brand is exclusive and high priced, the market size is, by design, very small. Given this situation, luxury retailers have two goals for their branding strategy: first, to build a brand that promotes luxury values; and second, to leverage that brand without diluting it to grow the market. There are two basic ways that luxury retailers can accomplish these goals: the "branded house" strategy, or the "house of brands" strategy.

Figure 5.2. Plotting Accessible Luxury on the Kahn Retailing Success Matrix

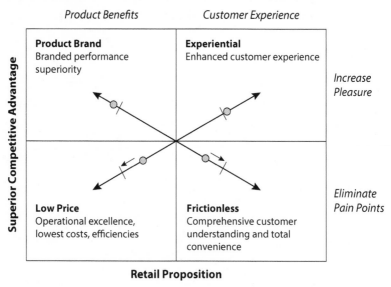

Product Benefits   *Customer Experience*

Superior Competitive Advantage

Product Brand
Branded performance superiority

Experiential
Enhanced customer experience

Increase Pleasure

Low Price
Operational excellence, lowest costs, efficiencies

Frictionless
Comprehensive customer understanding and total convenience

Eliminate Pain Points

Retail Proposition

Branded House Strategy

In the branded house strategy all of the items in the product line are branded with one brand name. Here the growth opportunity comes from having luxury branded products in lower-priced categories as well as in the usual higher-priced categories. For example, Chanel sells haute couture gowns for tens of thousands of dollars, but also has beauty products and fragrances that can be bought for under $100. While the Chanel makeup is more expensive than drugstore brands, it is clearly not as expensive as Chanel apparel, shoes, or purses.

Another method within the branded house strategy is to have subbrands or endorsed brands that are differentiated from the couture brand but still benefit from the brand halo. For example, Ralph Lauren has Purple Label that is higher-priced than Black Label, which in turn is higher priced than Polo. Within Armani, there is the higher-priced Giorgio Armani and the lower-priced Emporio

Armani. There are also lower-price diffusion product lines, which are in essence being promoted as separate brand names but are endorsed by the luxury house, such as AX by Armani.

House of Brands Strategy

The other approach is to have a house of brands, which is a portfolio of stand-alone brands that cater to different segments and different price points. This way one brand name does not contaminate or dilute another as they are all separate. European multinational luxury goods conglomerates like LVMH, Richemont, and Kering follow this strategy. For example, LVMH owns Louis Vuitton, Céline, Dior, Fendi, Givenchy, Loro Piana, Marc Jacobs, and many more. Kering owns Gucci, Bottega Veneta, Yves Saint Laurent, Alexander McQueen, and many others. Maintaining and building multiple brands is costlier than investing in just one brand, but there is mitigation of risk. Also, with the house of brands strategy growth frequently comes through acquisition as well as organically.

Product Line Decisions

Typically, when following the branded house strategy, the very top couture brands do not make money; rather, they exist to establish the credibility of the luxury brand name. The profitability comes from lower-priced branded goods that can sell in higher volumes. Outlets, which sell either out-of-season items, items for which supply exceeded demand, or made-for-outlet products at lower prices, can be very profitable because of the large volumes sold.

The trick is to leverage the brand name. For example, Ralph Lauren outlet products are valuable *because* Ralph Lauren is shown on the red carpet. To do this well, all brands within the label have to have a "Ralph" look, but the differences in the product tiers also have to be apparent.

When the Ralph strategy was at its peak, the brand succeeded because of a meticulous focus on its high-end image. The lower-end lines looked like the higher-end items, but everyone could tell the difference. The styles and materials were different; the lower end benefited from the brand name, but the higher-end brand name was not diluted. This type of strategy typically works well for brands that largely produce apparel, like Armani, Hugo Boss, and Ralph Lauren. Maintaining a full apparel line requires a large number of items (SKUs) to accommodate different size and style preferences. Discounting occurs if products do not sell and new seasonal products have to be brought in. That means it is very important for these luxury brands to forecast demand as accurately as possible so that there is not excess capacity at the end of the season.

Luxury retailers following the house of brands strategy typically have a higher percentage of accessories as opposed to apparel. Since the brands are separate there is no need to develop that brand voice across different price points. Forecasting accurate inventory levels for accessories is also much easier than for apparel because there are fewer sizes and colors. Accessories are more global, are less susceptible to seasonality and climate, and are easy to distribute broadly without adjustment. The downside here, of course, is the expense of maintaining so many different brands.

Accessible Luxury

Accessible luxury brands that are priced more affordably can be very profitable because they can reach larger audiences than true luxury brands can. However, these volumes come at the risk of longer-term brand dilution. Recently, many of the accessible luxury brands have been reexamining their brand strategies.

For example, Marc by Marc Jacobs was a diffusion brand that was launched in 2001 and offered products that were priced under $500. It was profitable but with economics that were less attractive than other European luxury brands that could command higher price premiums and could operate as vertical business models better able to fully consolidate their gross margins. In 2014, LVMH announced the decision to merge Marc and the main brand, Marc Jacobs, into one brand for the sake of simplification. Under this brand name they offered contemporary and premium products, exercised tighter control over wholesale distribution, and reduced off-price sales and promotions. This discipline, while protecting the brand, resulted in a loss of revenue—almost 50% in three years.

Similar woes befell Coach, whose sales plummeted in 2014 as its customers lost interest in its purses because of an overreliance on outlet sales and discounts. Victor Luis took over as CEO with a bold strategy to change the direction of the company. He purposely shrank the business and prioritized quality over mass-market quantity and discounting. He closed dozens of stores, ended online flash sales, and began to drop out of department stores. This strategy hurt top-line sales in the short term, but the goal is to build long-term profitability and stability.

In addition, Luis adopted the European luxury style of building brands through the house of brands strategy, acquiring Kate Spade and Stuart Weitzman. He also changed the name of the company to Tapestry, with Coach becoming one of the divisions of Tapestry. Although it is too early to assess the success of this strategy, other brands who had been overextended in the past, such as Gucci, have benefited from this type of more tightly controlled distribution, pricing, and design.

One accessible luxury brand that always had limited off-price discounting and a very tight control of outlet distribution from the get-go is Tory Burch. Hers is an American sportswear brand, which the company describes as classic yet modern, distinguished by a global and eclectic aesthetic. The brand launched in February 2004 as a full omnichannel model—both retail and e-commerce—which was very unusual at that time. Her brand support was always on social media; she did not wage classic advertising campaigns.

Burch's digital strategy included not only product descriptions, but articles, ideas, and other illustrations that supported her fashion. The story that unfolded on her social media was personal. The website reflects her personal history, starting with the life she lived growing up with her parents, Buddy and Reva Robinson (her most famous product, her ballet flats, are named after her mother), to her current life as a working mother.

Another unusual aspect of her business is the Tory Burch Foundation. This foundation supports the economic empowerment of women entrepreneurs and their families. All of this adds up to an authentic, intimate brand that is different from many others in this space, and builds loyalty, not through price discounts, but through an organic, resonating message.

Street and Urban "Luxury" Brand Strategies

Although not precisely similar to classic European royalty luxury, street and urban brands have some of the same characteristics. Supreme, launched in 1994, became the brand of choice for rebellious New York skaters and artists who were not only the customers but also employees. The brand worked with famous designers, artists, musicians, and photographers who all contributed to its unique identity. The first store opened in New York followed by a limited number of stores around the world. Others are following in this mold, including Hood by Air, Stüssy, and Raf Simons (the last is the namesake label that was launched in 1995 before Raf Simons took over as Dior's creative director in 2012).

Building a Luxury Customer Experience

Trends in fashion and luxury are changing. Historically, the power in the product line and design decisions has been controlled by the preeminent luxury department stores like Saks and Neiman Marcus. Then the luxury retail brands exercised the power of their brand names as the department stores started to fall out of favor. As this happened, the power in determining design decisions went to the celebrity creative directors and designers for each luxury brand. But more and more, consumers are leveraging their own power and demanding fashion *their* way.

As the retailing world becomes more competitive, and younger consumers are more empowered, customers want more than just a strong luxury brand product. These luxury retailers now need to offer more, and most are investing in luxurious customer experiences to build on their legacies. The luxury stores are becoming destinations in and of themselves. It is not just about shopping anymore; the stores now include entertainment and dining options.

Exclusivity

Scarcity and exclusivity are still important in designing these experiences. To make sure this occurs, many of the luxury stores, particularly in their flagship stores in tourist areas, control the number of people that are allowed in the store at any one time. In the big flagship stores in Milan, London, Hong Kong, or Paris, it is not uncommon to see the hot luxury brand of the moment (sometimes it's Chanel, or lately Gucci or Louis Vuitton) exercising strict crowd control.

This strategy has several advantages. First, it allows sales associates to devote exclusive attention to those customers, making sure they have the "luxury" experience they demand. Meanwhile, everyone else has to wait in line outside the store—and those lines only make the store seem more desirable and exclusive as well.

The Place to Be

Although not technically a luxury brand, Apple stores have always understood the value of extraordinary retail experiences. But, notably, they create the experiential value in a completely opposite way to the controlled-admission approach. Indeed, Apple stores are usually the most crowded ones in the mall.

Ron Johnson, who opened the first Apple retail store in 2001, created Genius Bars and friendly welcoming environments so customers could test all Apple products. The stores were immediately successful and made more money per square foot than Tiffany & Co. stores did.

More recently, Angela Ahrendts, former CEO of Burberry and now head of retail at Apple, announced Apple's new retail strategy to make the stores more like town squares or community centers. The idea is to create "gathering places" where consumers can hang out and perhaps take classes on coding, music, and photography. Here, the products are expensive, labeled with the "luxurious" brand name of

Apple, and the customer experience depends not on exclusive attention but rather being part of the "hip" community.

Customer Experience as a Gallery or Museum

Gucci is trying another approach. It recently announced the new Gucci Garden, which is located within a 14th-century palazzo in Florence. It costs 8 euros to enter, with half of the ticket sales donated to support restoration projects in Florence (where the brand was founded).

The first floor is free and sells Gucci products that are exclusive to the location. There is also a restaurant here. The second and third floors, which serve as a museum of the brand, are where the admission price is required. There are products that show off vintage and contemporary renderings of the logo, and displays that feature recurring themes in the brand's history. The idea is to immerse the customer in all things Gucci, allowing her to explore the brand narrative and legacy.

Louis Vuitton is experimenting with a similar concept. It has completely remodeled its flagship store in Chicago on Michigan Avenue to create a gallery setting. The outside façade includes layers of metal and wooden mesh and features an intricate bronze pattern based on an abstraction of the Damier pattern seen in many Vuitton products. The inside has design pieces and Peter Marino furniture selections.

The Drop Culture Experience

One way that Supreme secured its loyal base was to capitalize on the principle of scarcity and exclusivity in a different way. This brand was the originator of the "drop culture": Unlike other brands who introduce new products by season, Supreme releases 5 to 15 on a weekly basis.

Each week there is a drop, Supreme customers have to be at its stores on Thursday at exactly 11 a.m.—and even if they are, they may not leave with the product. The brand would deliver a certain number of items, deliberately limited so that not everyone would be able to get one. This would result in long lines of customers waiting outside the store for hours before the specified drop time. The products offered at the drops would sell out in minutes. The loyal customers who were lucky enough to get one would frequently share their bounty on social media. Even waiting in line had brand value; the line in some ways became the brand community, the brand experience. The *New York Times* called this the "cult of the line." These drops were very successful and traditional luxury brands noticed, which resulted in a collaboration between Supreme and Louis Vuitton in 2017, benefiting both brands.

Luxury Pop-Ups

Luxury retailers are also using pop-ups as opportunities to create experiences. This is their own version of the drop, in that they only exist for a limited amount of time. In 2017 Louis Vuitton opened a pop-up store on Madison Avenue in New York dedicated to the Louis Vuitton and Jeff Koons collaboration. The pop-up store covered 4,200 square feet and honored the original works of DaVinci, Van Gogh, Fragonard, and Rubens with enlarged prints and descriptions of the work on free-standing angled panels. The pop-up offered exclusive leather goods and accessories that came from this collaboration.

Tiffany & Co., Louis Vuitton, and Chanel all invested in pop-up stores for the 2017 holiday season. Chanel opened a pop-up called Coco Club for just one day and dedicated it to the brand's Boy-Friend watch. In addition to the product displays, there was a makeup studio, café, and library. A numerologist was available to give guests personalized readings.

Barneys New York is similarly adding more entertainment and exclusivity to its luxury retailing. It recently staged a two-day event called "thedrop@barneys," which had 30 brands providing capsule collections or single products along with designer appearances, activations, one of a kind experiences, and food and music.

Controlling Accessibility and Pricing

The paradox in luxury retailing is that unlike in most other retail transactions, where lower prices and convenience are attractive, here making the luxury product too easy to purchase undermines the value of the brand. This dilemma has resulted in luxury retailers being much slower than others to embrace digital platforms. This has not stopped other types of retailers from trying to fill that gap. Amazon, Alibaba, and JD.com all have third-party retailers flocking to their marketplace platforms and reselling branded goods at deep discounts or, worse still, selling unauthorized counterfeit products. Luxury brands are trying to crack down on the debilitating activity by buying back inventory from unauthorized sellers and working with big online players when possible to control the activity.

JD.com and Alibaba are starting to entice luxury brands by building luxury platforms where the brands can have tailored brand pages. JD.com has Toplife, which is designed to provide a white-glove concierge delivery service with same-day delivery. Alibaba has established a Luxury Pavilion, which again will help control luxury transactions.

Traditional Luxury Retailers Embracing E-Commerce Reluctantly

Only a few years ago, most luxury retailers pooh-poohed the importance of online commerce, but now many are reluctantly strategizing on ways to respond to the clear demands of consumers. Luxury online sales jumped by 24% in 2017, and estimates are that online sales will make up 25% of the luxury market by 2025.

Prada, Yves Saint Laurent, and others have publically stated goals to double their sales online in the next few years. The luxury watch industry has announced targeting efforts at young consumers through e-commerce resellers. Moving more slowly, Chanel's leadership team announced that it will sell its fragrances, beauty, and eyeglasses online—but not its exclusive outfits or handbags.

LVMH has launched an e-commerce platform called 24 Sèvres (named after the Paris street that Le Bon Marché is on). The site will carry more than 150 luxury women's apparel brands including Louis Vuitton, Christian Dior, Chloe, and Valentino. It will be the first time that major LVMH brands will be available on a multibrand web retailer. The main goal of this site will be to offer an experience that feels seamless and exclusive. There will be personal shopping assistants who will video chat with customers, and the site will sell products from other luxury companies, not just LVMH. The site is designed to look different from other e-commerce sites, with bold, beautiful imagery simulating window displays at high-end stores.

New E-Commerce Luxury Retailers Filling the Digital Gap

Even if the traditional luxury retailers are slow to sell their products online, other luxury retailers are filling that gap. Currently, the leader in global luxury e-commerce is the Yoox Net-a-Porter Group, which came about in 2015 through the merger of Yoox and Net-a-Porter.

This merger combined two complementary e-tailers. Yoox began by selling discounted, end-of-season luxury merchandise, and was a leader in back-end operations for other luxury retailers' e-commerce sites, such as the Kering brands, Armani, and Valentino. Net-a-Porter started with full-price merchandise and was known for its editorial content and customer experience. Yoox was a company of engineers; Net-a-Porter was a company of merchants and marketers. Together they operate a traditional wholesale model, buying and selling merchandise to customers. They take on inventory risk and high working capital requirements.

Yoox Net-a-Porter now has serious competition through Matches Fashion (the local chain of London-based luxury boutiques that is now an online force) and Farfetch, an online marketplace for 500 independent luxury boutiques and 200 brands that also owns the brick-and-mortar store Browns in London. Farfetch, an aggregator, doesn't hold inventory but rather works with individual fashion boutiques to sell to consumers. Farfetch offers services to the boutiques to help ensure the luxury experience by offering personal shoppers for its biggest spending customers. The advantage of being an aggregator is that it is easier to be profitable, as there is no responsibility for inventory. On the flip side, it is more difficult to guarantee that products will be in stock and delivered on time.

These e-commerce retailers are creating new ways to offer luxury service online. For example, Yoox Net-a-Porter introduced, "You Try, We Wait," which is a same-day try-on premium delivery service with at-home shopping consultations. Farfetch introduced the "Store of the Future," which is a suite of new technologies designed to help brands and boutiques bridge the worlds of online and offline. Experts are predicting that augmented reality will also be used to help merge the digital and physical worlds, creating a kind of "digital empathy."

Conclusion

Luxury continues to be a viable way to compete in this competitive retail world. While historically most high-end luxury retailers relied on the power of their exclusive, prestigious product brand names, this is no longer sufficient. These retailers have to continue to leverage their strengths while acknowledging changing consumer demands.

Most luxury retailers are experimenting with offering novel and desirable customer experiences that offer different types of luxury advantages. Although the central premise of luxury is scarcity and exclusivity, changes in consumer behavior are forcing luxury retailers to embrace the digital age and enter the Frictionless quadrant. New luxury retailers like Yoox Net-a-Porter and Farfetch are making great strides, and reluctantly some of the traditional retailers are developing e-commerce strategies of their own.

The critical strategy with respect to the lure of low price, though, will be to resist discounting and lowering prices as much as possible. Vigilant control of counterfeiting is also critical.

If all of these pieces can be managed, the luxury brand and experience strategy seems a viable way to compete against the Amazon effect—at least in the near future.

Chapter 6

Compete on Customer Experience: The Lure of Emotional and Sensory Engagement

In This Chapter: Kahn Retailing Success Strategy
- Retailers Whose Leadership Value Is to Offer Unique Customer Experiences
- Retailers Offering Great Customer Experiences as Their Second Leadership Quadrant

M ost retail experts believe that even with the massive growth in online shopping, the brick-and-mortar retail stores are not going away. Even Amazon is hedging its bets and getting into physical stores.

Stores still serve the critical purpose of allowing customers to touch and feel the product, to try things on, and to see how items look in real life. The social interaction with knowledgeable store associates is also valuable. Finally, the ability to take ownership of purchased items immediately is also beneficial in some circumstances.

The physical stores, though, will morph in response to changes in shopping behavior. Highly compelling in-store customer experiences will become more important as shoppers require additional reasons to visit the store. Brick-and-mortar retail space will evolve to include other experiences that complement shopping. Also, in-store technology will get better and better (and cheaper), and stores may start to include creative use of virtual reality, augmented reality, and real-time artificial-intelligence-driven algorithms that allow retailers to be actively responsive to customers' preferences and past behaviors.

Retailers who have prioritized the physical-store customer experience to create strategic differential advantages naturally fall into two categories.

First, there are the retailers who prioritize leadership in the Experiential quadrant as their chief strategic differentiation and then build on this leadership to maintain excellence in a second quadrant. An example here is Eataly, whose stated mission is "to create a place to learn about food, and through food, to learn about life." Building on this unique experience that includes cooking schools, restaurants, and gourmet food markets, Eataly offers leadership in the Product Brand quadrant by offering specialty foods from regional Italian producers that no one else does.

There are others who prioritize customer experience by recognizing the dynamic nature of experiences, so the variety or seasonality of the experiences becomes the reason to visit the store. An example here is the store Story, which changes its entire assortment every six weeks or so. Another example is the pop-up retailers who offer temporary stores to create interest. One of the originators of this idea is Spirit Halloween.

The second category of retailers are those who build leadership strategies in a different quadrant and then build on those leadership qualities to offer differentiating customer experiences. Examples here are retailers like Costco, with its club membership model, or T.J.Maxx, with its off-price strategy. Both retailers differentiate themselves with a low-price strategy but then bring customers into their stores for the fun of a treasure hunt experience—although these two retailers define treasure hunt differently.

Other retailers who build on a different leadership strategy but then leverage that to create awe-inspiring customer experiences include Sephora, whose loyalty program differentiates it in the Frictionless quadrant through its efforts to collect customer data and use it to create a peerless in-store customer experience. Another is Rebecca Minkoff, who built an accessible-luxury branded product

Figure 6.1. Plotting Unique Customer Experiences on the Kahn Retailing Success Matrix

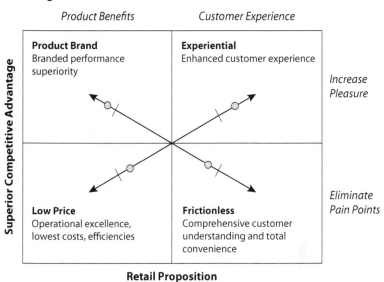

but differentiates her stores' experiences through state-of-the-art technology.

Retailers Whose Leadership Value Is to Offer Unique Customer Experiences

Part of the allure of unique experiences is that they are special and therefore not always available. Thus, like luxury strategies, these experiential retailers often do not meet fair value in the Frictionless quadrant and may not in Low Price either. Their leadership is first in the Experiential quadrant and then frequently followed by differentiated branded product. These ideas are plotted in Figure 6.1.

Eataly

Eataly is a food emporium that features fresh meats, cheese, seafood, an on-site bakery, wines, fresh pasta, an espresso bar, and gourmet

Italian specialty products, as well as full-service restaurants and a cooking school headed up by local celebrity chefs. There are currently only about three dozen locations worldwide, though the goal is to eventually have one store in every world capital. Eataly has an online presence as well, but that is clearly not its priority: As shown in Figure 6.1, convenience and accessibility are not its central objectives.

Oscar Farinetti started Eataly in Turin, Italy, in January 2007. He had been involved with the Slow Food movement for years and had made connections with many small-scale food producers and artisans in Italy. He built on these connections to provide Italian specialty products for his establishments that cannot be found anywhere else. In addition to the imported products and consistent with the Slow Food movement, 90% of the fresh products in Eataly establishments come from local areas. The emphasis on local products and local celebrity chefs make each Eataly unique.

The different components of the physical retail space provide complementary in-store consumer experiences, but they also provide synergy for the retailer. If the fresh product does not sell quickly enough it can be used in the restaurants before it spoils. Having a cooking school on the premises allows the customers to learn to appreciate the fine qualities of the foods and drinks that are offered, which should increase demand. The restaurants create buzz and traffic that leads people to the products sold in the market.

Eataly's store footprints are large; the newest one in Los Angeles is 67,000 square feet. Hence, the stores are often destinations. In keeping with this idea, Eataly recently launched a massive culinary theme park called Eataly World in Bologna, Italy. The food park has dozens of restaurants, on-site cows for cheese-making, truffle-hunting dogs, and culinary workshops and activities. The attraction is designed for tourists who travel for food experiences and want more than just fine dining. Part of the allure of the place is that it offers insights, learnings, and samples of all of the different regional foods within Italian culture.

Eataly is attempting to redefine retail. Rather than trying to maximize sales per square foot, which was the historic metric of success,

Eataly is defining itself in terms of the customer experience. It is more like a Starbucks or Disneyland in terms of prioritizing experience rather than a grocery store that tries to make profits by increasing frequency of purchase on low-margin items. Although Eataly's revenues are growing—the company predicted a 25% increase in sales in 2017 over 2016—executives stopped short of indicating whether it expected to be profitable. Nonetheless this model is spawning others; according to one estimate New York City now has more than 30 food halls by one definition or another. And many new malls are being built that are including some kind of gourmet food emporium.

Story

Another innovator who values experience over sales is Rachel Schectman, the CEO of New York City's retail-concept shop that is part store, part magazine, and part gallery. She only has one store, and it is only 2,000 square feet, but it has gotten a lot of attention for its untraditional approach to retail.

Every four to six weeks, Story completely changes its "story" or "theme," which means everything within the store is different, including all of the merchandise and the design. Schectman sells sponsorships to companies—typically big-name brands like NBC, Target, HP, and Nickelodeon—who are looking for alternative ways to connect with customers. The sponsors then work with her to provide the concept for their installation as well as the assortment of products to be sold, which are typically sourced from small businesses. Her store has been profitable since its inception.

Schectman's philosophy is that the future of retail customer experience has to include community and entertainment, and her aim is to provide engaging experiences. For example, for the installation that she did with Jet.com the Story was "Fresh." In addition to merchandise sold around the theme, Jet.com sponsored a multitude of events ranging from a conversation with a celebrity chef to cooking classes for children to a "make your own bitters" class. Each of these events brought together members of the community; Schectman reports there have even been couples who met at Story and started dating.

Like Eataly, the success metric here is not sales per square foot. In Schectman's case, she charges sponsorship money for creating a retail experience for a brand partner, as in an advertising or media contract. It is not about selling stuff, but about selling experiences.

Pop-Up Stores: Spirit Halloween

Another unique concept is the pop-up store, and Spirit Halloween was one of the first exponents of this in 1983. Spirit operates just the two months each year before Halloween—but those two months are lucrative, generating over $100 million in annual revenues. It's a tricky model because every year the store has to find new locations, fully staff those locations, and get the merchandise in place. Spirit opened roughly 1,300 temporary shops throughout the United States and Canada in 2017.

The idea behind a pop-up is temporary retail space that sells merchandise of any kind. They come in all shapes and sizes and are usually located in high foot-traffic areas. They can stay open from one day to three months. Although there are many reasons to open a pop-up, it is common to see them during holidays or when a brand is launching a new product. They offer uniqueness and novelty.

Luxury brands have seen the benefit of opening pop-up stores to help re-create their brand mystique. For example, Tiffany & Co. opened a pop-up store in Los Angeles in January 2018 designed to look like an oversized version of its iconic blue box. It stayed open for a month.

Just within that month of January 2018, a Google search indicated a plethora of other interesting pop-up stores, including a Zara pop-up in London to promote its online shopping experience; a Harry Potter pop-up in Causeway Bay in Hong Kong to capitalize on the demand for Harry Potter merchandise; a Gatorade pop-up in New York City to try and lure back users who have switched to other drinks; and a Prada pop-up store tour starting in Macau and going to other cities in China to try and create more excitement for the brand.

Pop-ups have benefited from the closing of many more traditional brick-and-mortar stores. It's much easier now to find a vacant spot in busy neighborhoods that will be just the right size for different uses. It's a win-win for landlords, too, as they take in rent for a space that would otherwise be empty. And pop-ups are usually designed to be fun, so they tend to bring traffic to the neighborhood.

Retailers Offering Great Customer Experiences as Their Second Leadership Quadrant

The second group of retailers who differentiate themselves on customer experience do so by building on a different primary leadership value. Although the strategies are different, Costco and T.J.Maxx (and other off-price retailers like Ross Stores and Burlington) are successful examples here. Their critical differential advantage is leadership in the Low Price quadrant, but they marry that strategy with an exciting treasure hunt in-store customer experience.

As an intrinsic part of this strategy, retailers do not hit fair value on branded product, either because they *cannot* advertise the brands they have by contract with those brands (off-price retailers) or because by design they offer limited breadth in product assortment (Costco). It is, ironically, this limitation that is the reason for the treasure hunt excitement. Further, because their models depend so much on the physical store, they have not prioritized the Frictionless quadrant and are either playing catch-up here (Costco) or deprioritizing it (off-price). These ideas are plotted on the Kahn Retailing Success Matrix in Figure 6.2.

Costco

The first Costco warehouse started in 1983 in Seattle as a membership club. Costco uses its buying clout to get great prices on items and then passes those cost savings on to its customers. In addition to having to pay an annual membership fee in order to shop, customers shop in warehouses where products are displayed on shipping pallets, and they have to buy in larger quantities than they would in a

Figure 6.2. The Treasure Hunt Model on the Kahn Retailing Success Matrix

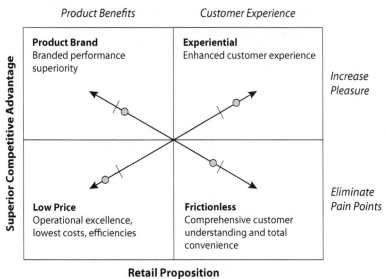

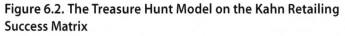

regular supermarket. In return, they are guaranteed the lowest prices in the market. This model attracts small businesses as well as individual consumers.

A typical Costco warehouse stocks about 4,000 items whereas a Walmart supercenter might carry 140,000 products. As a result, Costco only carries a limited number of brands in any particular category and offers no variety in sizes. The company runs very lean, with overhead costs at about 10% of revenue and profit margins at about 2%. The annual membership fees account for 80% of gross margin and 70% of operating income.

Costco's Leadership Strengths: Low Price
and Customer Experience

Primarily, Costco is seen as a low-price leader. In 2017 a price comparison done by JP Morgan in supermarket categories found that Costco prices on a per-unit basis were 30% cheaper than Walmart,

14% cheaper than Aldi, and 58% cheaper than Whole Foods, although Costco requires bulk purchases and the other supermarkets do not. Costco builds on this low-price advantage by offering a unique customer experience that serves to further motivate loyalty. This unique shopping experience occurs because customers are never quite sure what products will be offered at any time. Up to a fifth of Costco's stock is offered for a limited time only, and these items may be kept in the stores for only one week. Because of the uncertainty in assortment options, Costco trains its customers to buy something they like *when they see it*—because the next time they come it probably won't be there.

In addition to the treasure hunt experience, Costco store experiences are fun because of the tasting stations, which make the store feel like a party. In-store associates pass out trays of samples, supporting the social aspect of the store. The stores also draw customers into the physical plant because the warehouses sell gas at very low prices.

None of these physical store experiences—the treasure hunt, product sampling, or filling a car up with gas—can be adequately had online, so Costco has historically been a laggard in that space.

Costco Looks to Reach Fair Value in the Other Quadrants: Brand and Online

In the Product Brand quadrant, even though Costco offers a limited assortment, it is possible for it to achieve fair value here for several reasons. First, as mentioned, the limited assortment can offer excitement in the form of a treasure hunt. Second, in a world of far too much choice, having limited choice of high-quality goods may actually be beneficial; Costco has a reputation for having very high-quality brands, so its limited assortment is almost viewed as a curated assortment, where the customer cannot go wrong because everything is of high quality. Finally, Costco's product image is strong because of its respected private-label Kirkland Signature brand.

Since 1995 Costco has used its Kirkland Signature products to attract shoppers. The brand is very high quality with a low price.

About 25% of annual sales come from Kirkland products, and that percentage is growing. Further, Costco uses the possibility of its introducing a Kirkland product as incentive to make sure the national brands are selling at their lowest price.

When Costco considers developing new products under the Kirkland brand, it looks for products that are top sellers that it believes can be sold for at least 20% less. If Costco decides to develop a private-label version, it looks to do so without eroding quality, and it is careful to make products that are slightly different from branded versions.

Costco plays fair; before going with a private brand, it gives the brand-name supplier the chance to make the Kirkland version too. For example, Costco asked P&G (Pampers) and Kimberly-Clark (Huggies) to make private Kirkland-branded diapers. Kimberly-Clark agreed and now Huggies are the only branded version sold on Costco shelves, in addition to the Kirkland brand.

In the Frictionless quadrant, Costco is definitely playing catch-up. Although it has a very strong and sticky membership base, it has two liabilities that suggest it is vulnerable in this quadrant. First, a 2017 Morgan Stanley study estimated that almost half of Costco shoppers are also members of Amazon Prime.

Second, Costco has been very slow to respond to the e-commerce threat. Recently, this has changed as Costco grocery has partnered with Instacart and also offers a limited number of buy-online-pickup-in-store items. Costco also launched CostcoGrocery, a service that offers two-day delivery on shelf-stable products ordered through its website.

These innovations increased e-commerce sales by 43.5% in the first quarter of the fiscal year 2017. Even with these increases in e-commerce sales, however, these revenues are still a very small part of overall sales, and Costco continues to ride on its success as a fun and interesting place to shop in the physical warehouses.

How Will Costco Fare in the Future against Amazon?

As of the end of 2017, Costco's sales numbers were good, even as Amazon was threatening to come into grocery. During the critical

Thanksgiving shopping period last year, Costco's sales rose 13.2% year over year, even in light of Amazon's rapid growth. Its same-store sales rose 10.8% overall during the month of November, Costco's growth was seen across many categories including appliances, tables, computers, auto, tires, sporting goods, office sales, jewelry, apparel, and domestics. Analysts are suggesting that Costco may be insulated from Amazon with its unique model, noting that store traffic is strong and membership renewal rates are at 90%.

One big question, however, is whether digitally native millennials and Gen Z'ers will be as into the physical store advantages that Costco offers as their parents are. In general, the core club customer is older, has a family, and lives in a house. There is some indication that younger consumers are not as keen on Costco's stores because of the response to an online competitor, Boxed, which started in 2013.

Boxed's mission is to deliver bulk goods to shoppers who don't live near a wholesale club or don't have a car to get to one. But the site attracted other shoppers too—those who just didn't want to go in person to the club to buy staples, even though the clubs were accessible. Costco reports that the average age of its customers is dropping, and that it is actively trying to attract millennials. This remains an open question.

T.J.Maxx, Burlington, and Ross Stores

T.J.Maxx, Burlington, and Ross Stores are all stores that have been identified as "off-price," and they all follow a similar model. They buy products in bulk at very good prices and then pass these lower prices on to the consumers. They are "everyday low price" and do not discount. They make profits from volume; they sell lots of goods and they sell them fast.

These retailers buy two types of products for their stores: (1) true closeout products (i.e., branded products that were created to sell at full price in other stores but didn't sell for one reason or the other); and (2) products that are made specifically for the off-price channel, designed to be sold at the discounted prices.

The first group are true bargains, often selling at 20% to 60% below retail price, and contribute to the treasure hunt feel. Unlike at Costco, in these stores there are only a few of any specific designs and/or sizes in each store, but the stores offer very broad assortments with tons of variety that changes frequently.

These retailers are "fashion" retailers; they are not in the business of selling other retailers' losing bets. They have large numbers of buyers who study the trends. Unlike traditional fashion retailers, they don't have to make a bet at the beginning of the season; rather, they can buy closed-out products and samples during the season when they have better evidence about what is selling.

The key to success with these retailers is to be attuned to fashion. They invest in significant buyer training. The buyers buy most weeks of the year (not just seasonably) and they are negotiating significant amounts of money in each transaction. Knowing when to buy is as important as what to buy. Most of their items turn over quickly.

The second group of products—those specifically made for these chains—can also follow fashion trends quickly. If the off-price buyers see a hot trend, they can negotiate with manufacturers to have merchandise made for them directly. Some of the vendors will produce an excess of hot items knowing that the off-price buyers will take them. The advantage to the vendors is that the off-price retailers will buy in volume, which will help economies of scale. And these off-price retailers will spread that product across their stores so there is not a lot of supply in any one place. These arrangements are typically not publicized, which is beneficial for both.

All of these stores have a large physical footprint, which makes for very broad, but not deep, assortments. T.J.Maxx stores, for example, may cover 23,000 square feet of retail space. It sources from more than 16,000 vendors around the world. Burlington stores are even bigger, sometimes as large as 80,000 square feet, but they are being scaled back to probably half of that.

Customers of off-price retailers come to the store not knowing what to expect, but they know if they find a great bargain they have to buy it right away because it won't be there the next time. This provides a real sense of urgency and excitement, which helps to turn over the inventory quickly. Fast-turning inventory increases the frequency at which consumers come into the store.

No Plans for Online Platforms

This is a shopping experience that doesn't translate to online shopping easily. From the consumer side, the shopping experience would not translate to a small computer screen (or worse mobile phone), where you need to know what you are looking for. In a physical store, you can scan the store, see things in peripheral vision, and find treasures accidentally. Online search is far more focused.

From the retailer side, there are disincentives to try to replicate the process online because of the rapid turnover in the stores. This suggests that photographing the rapidly changing inventory would be difficult, and without extensive description of each of the items, seeing and trying on the product physically in the stores becomes more important. To the degree it is difficult to fully describe the items quickly, returns are a much bigger issue—let alone the costs of delivery, which in this model the consumer bears. Further, manufacturers will not allow easy identification of their brand products, so online search is prohibited. All of this makes it difficult to see how this type of retailing will successfully move online.

Successful Numbers

This sector is posting strong results, with steady sales and earnings growth. Although this segment is very successful, the off-price model has been hard to get right; many have failed in the past. Syms overextended; Loehmann's couldn't scale; Century 21 is very good but small; and Filene's Basement couldn't scale and found itself overextended.

The key to success here is the supply chain and distribution. A successful retailer in this model needs huge, fully automated distribution centers in the right places. It needs to buy the product from all over the world and then distribute it efficiently and effectively to all of its stores. Most of these retailers have a "door-to-floor" approach, eliminating the need for backroom storage. It is key to have rapid turnover of inventory in the stores, to keep assortment fresh, and to encourage consumers to keep coming back. They also need to be able to store a lot of inventory if necessary.

Risks to the Model in the Future

Although this model has been very successful for the big three— T.J.Maxx, Ross, and Burlington—success brings competition and the large department stores are noticing. They are prioritizing their own off-price offerings and opening up new stores. Further, as technology and artificial intelligence makes it easier to predict what consumers will want, demand forecasts should be more accurate and there may be less full-price inventory for sale.

Some analysts have speculated that there may be competition from online secondhand retailers like thredUP and Everything But The House. But that seems unlikely for many reasons. First, secondhand clothing definitely has a time lag, which may matter for fashionistas. Second, there are some consumers who just don't like the idea of wearing clothing that strangers have worn before. Probably more important, though, are the supply-side costs like shipping costs, inventory costs, distribution, photographing the items, and returns, which would make it difficult for this type of channel to compete effectively.

Other Retailers Building Strong Customer Experiences on Other Leadership Strengths

Finally, there are other retailers who provide amazing customer experiences based on strengths in other quadrants. Sephora built a strong loyalty program and has leveraged that online expertise to craft a can't-miss store experience. Rebecca Minkoff built a strong, accessible luxury brand and is further differentiating by taking the lead in state-of-the-art in-store technology.

Figure 6.3. Plotting In-Store Customer Experience on the Kahn Retailing Success Matrix

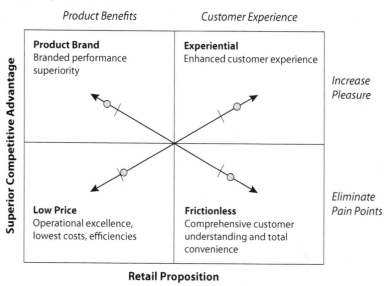

Both of these specialty retailers are competing effectively with very strong branded product and online, frictionless strategies. They excel at customer experience and hit fair value on price, with an aim to motivate on value rather than on discounting. These ideas are plotted in Figure 6.3.

Sephora

Sephora, owned by LVMH, is a fully integrated omnichannel experience with a very loyal customer base. The store is a makeup playground. Consumers come into the store to experiment with makeup, skin care products, perfumes, and anything beauty related. The store associates are there to help and educate. They are not on commission.

The in-store experience is connected with customers' online accounts, so there is a record of previous purchases, making color matches easy to reproduce. Also, all purchases are recorded to a robust loyalty program, which not only allows for appropriate recommendations and announcements of personalized new products, but also awards bonus points that lead to fun beauty gifts that keep the customer addicted.

Although online experience may be useful for repurchasing stock items, the beauty purchase is especially conducive to an in-store experience, as most people like to try on products before buying. And new is fun; in addition to changing fashions and styles, the dream of finding the perfect product that will keep you forever young and beautiful is enticing.

Sephora's combination of a well-run loyalty program (with well-timed and well-designed bonus gifts) and a fun in-store environment is intoxicating. The stores are always crowded, and I have personally seen women standing outside of a closed Sephora store, literally crying that they didn't make it there in time.

Sephora is also continually experimenting with new concepts to keep in-store environments novel and fresh. In 2015 it introduced the TIP (Teach, Inspire, Play) concept that featured makeup classes with a completely interactive experience designed for innovation and experimentation. Makeup stations in the store had sensory and color technology to help customers learn about new possibilities. Sephora also experiments with augmented reality, which allows customers to try on makeup virtually.

The Sephora experience is also about social interaction. For example, there is a robust Beauty Insider community where customers talk with each other about products and fashion, and anything and everything related to beauty. In just the first few months after its launch, the program had 100,000 live chats and more than 20,000 photos were shared.

Sephora has also opened small Sephora Studio stores, which are designed to have a neighborhood feel. Here the emphasis is on intimacy and building relationships between the customer and store associates, which encourages even more repeat visits.

Is Sephora Vulnerable to the Amazon Threat?

Amazon is rumored to be looking at beauty in addition to fashion. It could probably improve its app to copy some of Sephora's features, and there may be possibilities that could be realized with the photography feature of Amazon Echo. Effective price competition could possibly steal away repurchase orders. But until Amazon prioritizes the experiential and social in-store experience that Sephora excels at, Sephora's customers will likely stay put.

In addition to Amazon, there is plenty of other competition in this segment. The department stores historically owned a lot of this market, especially at the higher end where Sephora competes. At the lower-price points, drugstores, supermarkets, and mass merchandisers can compete with better prices but little opportunity for in-store experimentation. Ulta is doing extremely well in combining both high- and low-priced goods with a compelling in-store environment that includes salons and a strong loyalty program. There are also many startups eyeing this space, including Birchbox and the upcoming and fast-growing Glossier.

Rebecca Minkoff

Rebecca Minkoff is an accessible luxury global brand that spans apparel, handbags, footwear, jewelry, and accessories (including men's accessories under the label Uri Minkoff). The woman behind the brand is unique in the accessible luxury world in that she is positioning her line as the place where tech and fashion merge. As part of this messaging, she is transforming the customer experience in her stores. Rebecca Minkoff stores were among the first to attempt to transform a physical store into something more like a website—both in providing data as the customer needs it and in capturing customer preferences by observing behaviors throughout the store.

Back in 2014, Rebecca Minkoff's New York City and San Francisco stores featured state-of-the art tech that allowed this website-like interaction. As customers entered the store and logged on to the brand's app, they encountered a large interactive screen that allowed them to interact with Rebecca herself for recommendations based on their personal preferences and past behaviors. In addition to the recommendations, they could order a drink, reserve a fitting room, find out about the newest items in the store, and more.

All of the merchandise in the store was tagged with RFID technology. When customers brought any item into the dressing room, this technology automatically had the items that were brought in appear on the "magic mirror" in front of them. This served two purposes. First, it allowed the retailer to record what items were taken into the dressing room, information that heretofore had been lost. This information is akin to online retailers recording what items make it into an online cart, even if in the end customers do not purchase the items.

Second, based on the items the customer brought in, recommendations could be made as to what might go with these items. Further, customers could request different sizes or colors just by touching the mirror, and a sales associate would bring the requested items. It was similarly easy when the customer was ready to pay. In addition to the incredible convenience, all of this data were recorded.

The in-store technology increased customers' time spent in store and boosted clothing sales. Of the customers who tried things on in these fitting rooms, 30% requested additional items to be brought in by an associate via the mirror's touch screen. The information also gave Rebecca Minkoff useful market research data as to what items were tried on together, and how many different sizes/colors were sampled.

More recently Rebecca Minkoff has been experimenting with virtual reality, eager to be the first brand to sell to customers in a virtual reality world. It has been working with Store No. 8, Walmart's tech incubation arm. The experiments have been helpful in figuring out the best layouts in stores to most benefit customers—this can be done much more cheaply in virtual reality than actually experimenting in physical stores.

In sum, Rebecca Minkoff is an example of a retailer using technology in the customer experience as a differentiator. It is beneficial in promoting Minkoff's brand—many articles and blogs have been written about her endeavors—it provides a superior customer experience that drives traffic to the store, and it enables the collection of customer data within the physical store.

Conclusion

All of the retailers in this chapter have excelled in customer experience. As with branded products, each experience is unique, and that is the appeal. Like luxury, sometimes these experiences are special *because* they are hard to access, rare, or scarce—the opposite of the convenient and frictionless experience, Amazon's forte. Many of the retailers who prioritize physical customer experience do not prioritize online e-commerce (although Sephora and Rebecca Minkoff are exceptions here).

Of course, good ideas are always copied, so competition might be around the corner. Second, experiences that are considered fun, like the fashion shopping experience, might change over time. Finally, although currently not the case, perhaps in the future virtual reality will make these experiences reproducible at home.

As always, cost-benefit analysis will be necessary to measure whether the investment in in-store experiences delivers long-term returns. But at the very least, there is evidence that if retailers build the excitement, customers will come.

Conclusion

The retailing industry is fundamentally changing. The United States, which has been "over-stored" for a while, is currently experiencing an unprecedented number of stores closing. Partly causing this is the tremendous growth in online shopping. Another change is the pervasive use of the mobile phone for 24-hour connectivity that allows retailers and consumers to bridge the gap between the offline and online universes.

There are also new models of retailing that are being developed by innovative startups. These include subscription models, brick-and-mortar retail stores used as showrooms rather than selling spaces, and the new renting and sharing paradigms. In addition to all of this industry disruption, there are macro socioeconomic trends occurring, including a new generation of digitally savvy shoppers; incredible technology advances for in-store retailing; the advent of big data, artificial intelligence, and virtual reality; and a reaction to the Great Recession that has made consumers more price sensitive.

Kahn Retailing Success Matrix

The purpose of this book has been to share a framework, the Kahn Retailing Success Matrix, to help make sense of all this change. The Kahn Retailing Success Matrix allows for the systematic mapping of various retailing strategies on the same axes so they can be compared easily. This provides a common vocabulary for discussing different successful strategic alternatives. It also allows for measurement on the underlying axes over time and provides a graphing tool such that progress can be measured.

Strategically, the framework has several important prescriptions.

1. *It is critical to be the best at a one leadership value and then leverage that leadership value to be the best at something else.* It is not okay to be "good enough" at lots of things. In very competitive industries, like retailing has become, it is first necessary to become the best at one of the quadrant strategies, and then leverage that leadership advantage to become the best at a second leadership value. I call this the "two-quadrant winning" strategy. Trying to be "the best" at too many things though results in suboptimality, so it is necessary to focus and maintain leadership in two core strengths, and not try to be good at everything. Losing that focus and letting your leadership strengths get diluted is disastrous.

2. *You have to meet fair value on everything where you aren't the best.* The implication here is that while retailers do need to meet customers' minimal expectations on aspects that do not deliver to their strengths, they do not have to be the market leaders in those areas; however, they cannot be subpar either.

3. *Customers' fair-value expectations are constantly increasing as the market gets more competitive.* While retailers only need to be at fair value at activities that are not their strengths, these fair-value goals are moving targets. Smart competitors, like Amazon, are constantly raising the table stakes.

Shopping Is an Omnichannel Experience

The shopping revolution is not about the movement from physical stores to online shopping. Rather, consumers now expect seamless integration across *all* channels. The data from the offline, mobile, and online experiences have to be merged, and progressive retailers must use that comprehensive data to individualize their real-time store experiences. Shoppers expect to be able to search online and pick up in the stores, or search in the store and buy online. This is the new "normal."

Metrics Need to Change

In this new world of retailing, standard metrics like sales per square foot, profit/loss by channel, traffic count, and basket size are not the only metrics to consider—and may not even be the most appropriate. Home Depot executives, for example, are considering new metrics, such as impact to brand impression, digital purchase intent, and customer convenience and experience measures.

And it is not just metrics in the store. We are definitely moving to more of a platform model, where consumers can transact whenever they want across several channels: physical store, mobile, online, social media, or the Internet of Things. This means that retailers should strive to have ownership of the customer experience across as many channels and functions as possible, and many are failing to measure this.

Kurt Salmon consultants label this omission as the "digital experience gap." They argue that one important metric to consider is "share of home," or share of the home ecosystem (e.g., Amazon's Alexa or Apple's Siri).

Here the retailer that can ultimately control the shopping list has a real advantage. If a consumer is recording all of his or her household needs with Alexa on Amazon Echo, then Amazon is in the driver's seat. Another goal is to increase the frequency of interaction with the consumer, so more data can be collected and mined to better understand what customers want and need. This desire for more interaction with the customer has motivated savvy retailers like Amazon to get into other businesses such as media, entertainment products, or Amazon Home Services.

Can Traditional Retailers Rebound?

One of the implications of the Kahn Retailing Success Matrix is that retailers who do not lead in two quadrants are susceptible to falling retail sales. We are certainly seeing this as traditional retailers such as Macy's, Sears, and Gap close hundreds of stores and are being forced to continually discount slow-moving inventory. As J.Crew's ex-CEO Mickey Drexler, once lauded as the "merchant prince," said about his core customer: "She's loyal as hell until we go wrong. Then she wants it on sale."

The traditional retailers are "stuck in the middle." Not only are they not the leaders, but traditional retailers have failed to meet the ever-increasing customer expectations that are set by their more progressive competitors.

These traditional retailers are failing in all four quadrants. Amazon and other online retailers have captured sales from customers who now demand the convenience of online shopping and speedy delivery. Sephora and Ulta are luring away the cosmetic and beauty shoppers who crave more interactive and social in-store environments. Vertical fashion brands are shying away from selling their goods through the traditional department store and retailing platforms and are selling their branded products directly to the end user. Finally, the price-sensitive and bargain-loving shoppers are attracted to the everyday low-price treasure hunt experiences of the off-price retailers.

Can these traditional retailers come back? It's possible. Their dreary store experiences have to be updated. They have to get to the state-of-the art in e-commerce. But that's not enough. They then have to give customers a reason to come to them; they have to find their own leadership strategies.

Probably the best bet for these mainstream retailers is for them to win once again in the branded product and open new channels to compete in the Low Price quadrant. Macy's new CEO has promised that Macy's will be the new "fashion authority." If he can deliver on that promise, that could bring their loyal shoppers back. Macy's has also opened their own off-price, treasure hunt experience with their new Backstage stores. Again, if they can move to a leadership strategy here, they could be a viable player.

Similarly, Gap is closing many of their Gap and Banana Republic stores, which are often "stuck in the middle" with no real leadership positioning, and are reinvesting in Old Navy, which competes effectively in the Low Price quadrant with trending fashion, and in Athleta, which offers a branded product that appeals to a targeted segment. To stay current, these chains will have to adopt some of the strategies from their "fast fashion" competitors and move to fast and flexible supply chains so they can better deliver to fast-moving trends as they are happening.

These are certainly steps in the right direction, but the key question is: Can they succeed and become the leaders they once were, or will it be too little, too late?

Appendix: Measuring Fair-Value Thresholds

As noted in chapter 1, fair-value expectations are plotted as hash marks on each axis, as shown in Figure 1.3. The customers' expectations are all equidistant from the origin, but this does not have to be the case. The further out the customers' threshold expectations are from the origin, the higher the expectations are on that dimension, representing a more competitively difficult market in which to compete and win.

To measure these fair-value thresholds, dedicated market research should be conducted to see what consumers are expecting. For example, for the brand and price dimensions, standard choice-based conjoint analysis can be conducted for the category to determine the relative importance of brand and price in the product decisions for each strategic consumer segment and the relative utility for different price and brand values. Market research can also determine the minimum acceptable values on each of these axes.

For the customer experience dimensions, this is less common to measure. However, the same types of market research tools can be used. For example, for the Frictionless quadrant, conjoint techniques can be used to determine the importance weights of speedy delivery times, recommendation systems, and usability of apps or voice recognition devices. In addition, objective measures such as average service times and others can be recorded.

Probably the most difficult expectation to measure is the Experiential quadrant, simply because these experiences will be idiosyncratic and novel almost by definition. In this case, benchmarking techniques could perhaps substitute. For example, in the beauty business, customers' evaluation of competitors' store experiences can be used. The minimum threshold could be defined as the average experience score. It may also be the case that evaluation of this dimension might be reflected in the value that the consumers place on the retailer's brand name (e.g., Sephora or Eataly). If that is the case, then these values can be evaluated similarly to the way product brand-name importance weights and ratings are measured using conjoint analysis. Albert Vita, the director of strategy insights and visual merchandising at Home Depot, has suggested some other creative measures for this quadrant such as inspiration per square foot and convenience for associates in delivering on customer experience.

After the customers' expectations are plotted, then the firm's own position can be plotted on these axes, relative to these fair-value or threshold expectations. Is the firm delivering below or above customers' expectations on each of these dimensions?

One way to track whether the firm is meeting customer expectations over time is to use an adaptation of Bain's Net Promoter Scores (NPS) process. For example, retailers could compute NPS scores on each dimension: fair prices, convenience, enjoyable shopping experience, desirable brands. This would result in indices that range from −100 to 100, which can be used as proxies for gauging customers' overall satisfaction with the company's performance. To assess the relative competitive advantage the scores of close competitors can also be measured.

References

Introduction

Andrews, Travis M., "America Is 'Over-Stored' and Payless ShoeSource Is the Latest Victim," *Washington Post*, April 5, 2017, accessed February 24, 2018, https://www .washingtonpost.com/news/morning-mix/wp/2017/04/05/america-is-over-stored-and -payless-shoesource-is-the-latest-victim/?utm_term=.4aee285104d5.

BI Intelligence, "Amazon Accounts for 43% of US Online Retail Sales," *Business Insider*, February 3, 2017, accessed on February 24, 2018, http://www.businessinsider.com /amazon-accounts-for-43-of-us-online-retail-sales-2017-2.

Chitrakorn, Kati, "5 Technologies Transforming Retail in 2018," *The Business of Fashion*, January 19, 2018, accessed February 24, 2018, https://www.businessoffashion .com/articles/fashion-tech/5-technologies-transforming-retail.

Clark, Patrick, and Dorothy Gambrell, "These Cities Have Too Many Stores, and They're Still Building," *Bloomberg*, June 12, 2017, accessed February 25, 2018, https:// www.bloomberg.com/news/articles/2017-06-12/what-s-killing-american-retail-take-a -look-at-this-chart-for-a-start.

Farner, Shawn, "How Big Data is Changing the Retail Industry," *Disruptor Daily*, November 10, 2017, accessed February 24, 2018, https://www.disruptordaily.com/big -data-changing-retail-industry/.

Green, Dennis, and Megan Harney, "More than 8,000 Store Closures Were Announced in 2017—Here's the Full List," *Business Insider*, December 20, 2017, accessed February 24, 2018, http://www.businessinsider.com/stores-closures-announced-in-2017 -2017-12/#radioshack-1430-stores-1.

Howard, Robert, Jack Horst, Michele Orndorff, and Paul Schottmiller, *Surviving the Brave New World of Food Retailing: A Roadmap to Relevance for the Future for Food Retailers*, Kurt Salmon/Coca Cola Retailing Research Council, 2016, accessed February 24, 2018, https://www.ccrrc.org/2017/01/26/surviving-brave-new-world-food-retailing-roadmap -relevance-future.

Hyken, Shep, "Sixty-Four Percent of U.S. Households Have Amazon Prime," *Forbes*, June 17, 2017, accessed February 24, 2018, https://www.forbes.com/sites/shephyken /2017/06/17/sixty-four-percent-of-u-s-households-have-amazon-prime/#6b2f48784586.

Medal, Andrew, "4 Things You Need to Know about Gen Z's Shopping Habits," *Inc.*, November 27, 2017, accessed February 25, 2018, https://www.inc.com/andrew-medal /how-to-give-gen-z-ers-shopping-experience-they-want.html.

"Navigating the Digital Experience Paradox," *Kurt Salmon*, September 26, 2016, accessed February 25, 2018, http://www.kurtsalmon.com/en-us/Retail/vertical-insight/1626/Navigating-the-Digital-Experience-Paradox.

Pandolph, Stephanie, and Jonathan Camhi, "Amazon Prime Subscribers Hit 80 Million," *Business Insider*, April 27, 2017, accessed on February 24, 2018, http://www.businessinsider.com/amazon-prime-subscribers-hit-80-million-2017-4.

Pickard, Katie, "Generation Z and Its 3 Most Important Consumer Behaviors," *Precision Dialogue*, February 6, 2017, accessed February 24, 2018, http://www.precisiondialogue.com/generation-z-consumer-behaviors/.

Reda, Susan, "21 Ways Amazon Changed the Face of Retail," *Stores Magazine*, September 2016, pp. 30–33.

Reynolds, Cormac, "5 Ways Big Data Is Changing Retail and How We Shop and Sell," *Data Floq*, November 19, 2015, accessed February 24, 2018, https://datafloq.com/read/5-ways-big-data-changing-retail-shop-sell/1682.

Sonsev, Veronika, "Retail Technology and Marketing Trends on the Rise for 2018," *Fortune*, January 22, 2018, accessed February 24, 2018, https://www.forbes.com/sites/veronikasonsev/2018/01/22/retail-technology-and-marketing-trends-on-the-rise-for-2018/#10b5f7ec64c0.

Thomas, Lauren, "Bankruptcies Will Continue to Rock Retail in 2018. Here's What You Need to Watch," *CNBC*, December 13, 2017, accessed February 24, 2018, https://www.cnbc.com/2017/12/13/bankruptcies-will-continue-to-rock-retail-in-2018-watch-these-trends.html.

Thompson, Derek, "What in the World Is Causing the Retail Meltdown of 2017?," *The Atlantic*, April 10, 2017, accessed February 26, 2018, https://www.theatlantic.com/business/archive/2017/04/retail-meltdown-of-2017/522384/.

Treacy, Michael, and Fred Wiersema, *The Discipline of Market Leaders: Choose Your Customers, Narrow Your Focus, Dominate Your Market* (Reading, MA: Addison-Wesley, 1995).

Wertz, Boris, "The Next Big E-Commerce Wave: Vertically Integrated Commerce," *TechCrunch*, September 29, 2012, accessed February 24, 2018, https://techcrunch.com/2012/09/29/the-next-big-e-commerce-wave-vertically-integrated-commerce/.

Chapter 1

Howard, Robert, Jack Horst, Michele Orndorff, and Paul Schottmiller, *Surviving the Brave New World of Food Retailing: A Roadmap to Relevance for the Future for Food Retailers*, Kurt Salmon/Coca Cola Retailing Research Council, 2016, accessed February 24, 2018, https://www.ccrrc.org/2017/01/26/surviving-brave-new-world-food-retailing-roadmap-relevance-future.

Krantz, Matt, "Amazon Just Surpassed Walmart in Market Cap," *USA Today*, July 23, 2015, accessed March 30, 2018, https://www.usatoday.com/story/money/markets/2015/07/23/amazon-worth-more-walmart/30588783/.

Loeb, Walter, "Macy's and Other Retailers Need Merchants Who Will Step Out to Win," *Forbes*, July 6, 2017, accessed February 24, 2018, https://www.forbes.com/sites

/walterloeb/2017/07/06/macys-and-every-other-retailer-as-well-needs-merchants-who
-will-step-out-to-win/#18530641af36.

"Mixed Feelings: How Shoppers Think about Brick-and-Mortar," *eMarketer Retail*,
May 3, 2017, accessed February 24, 2018, https://retail.emarketer.com/article/mixed
-feelings-how-shoppers-think-about-brick-and-mortar/590a4d28ebd400097ccd5f8b.

"Navigating the Digital Experience Paradox," *Kurt Salmon*, September 26, 2016,
accessed February 25, 2018, http://www.kurtsalmon.com/en-us/Retail/vertical-insight
/1626/Navigating-the-Digital-Experience-Paradox.

Ruff, Corinne, "7 Retail Execs Envision the Future of Stores," *Retail Dive*, February 13,
2018, accessed February 24, 2018, https://www.retaildive.com/news/7-retail-execs
-envision-the-future-of-stores/516795/.

Treacy, Michael, and Fred Wiersema, *The Discipline of Market Leaders: Choose Your Customers, Narrow Your Focus, Dominate Your Market* (Reading, MA: Addison-Wesley, 1995).

Wahba, Phil, "Amazon Will Make Up 50% of All U.S. E-Commerce by 2021,"
Fortune, April 20, 2017, accessed March 30, 2018, http://fortune.com/2017/04/10/
amazon-retail/.

Chapter 2

Amazon.com, "Jeff Bezos' 2016 Letter to Shareholders," April 17, 2017, accessed April 3,
2018, https://www.amazon.com/p/feature/z6o9g6sysxur57t.

Amazon.com, "Powering Earth's Best Customer Service Experience," accessed March 30,
2018, https://www.amazon.jobs/en-gb/team/customer-service-technology.

Amazon.com, "Working at Amazon," accessed March 30, 2018, https://www.amazon
.com/p/feature/cdkk293z8nzm7q8.

"Amazon Strategy Teardown: Building New Business Pillars in AI, Next-Gen Logistics,
and Enterprise Cloud Apps," *CB Insights*, 2017, accessed February 24, 2018, https://
www.cbinsights.com/research/report/amazon-strategy-teardown/.

Broida, Rick, "You Just Got Your First Amazon Dash Button, Now What?" *CNET*,
December 8, 2017, accessed February 24, 2018, https://www.cnet.com/how-to/you-just
-got-your-first-amazon-dash-button-now-what/.

Chafkin, Max, "Amazon Needs to Watch What It Eats," *Bloomberg*, July 31, 2017,
accessed February 26, 2018, https://www.bloomberg.com/news/articles/2017-07-31
/amazon-needs-to-watch-what-it-eats.

CNBC, "Amazon's $13.7 Billion Bet on Online Grocery Ordering Hasn't Convinced
Shoppers to Stay Home," *US Stock Info*, October 17, 2017, accessed February 24, 2018,
https://stockinfo.us/2017/10/17/cnbc-amazon-s-13-7-billion-bet-on-online-grocery
-ordering-hasn-t-convinced-shoppers-to-stay-home/.

Gabor, Deb, "How the Amazon-Sears Deal Could Make the Smart Home a Reality,"
Fortune, July 26, 2017, accessed February 25, 2018, http://fortune.com/2017/07/26
/amazon-sears-kenmore-smart-home/.

Gasparro, Annie, and Laura Stevens, "Amazon's Grocery Ambitions Spell Trouble for Big
Food Brands," *Wall Street Journal*, June 26, 2017, accessed February 26, 2018, https://

www.wsj.com/articles/amazons-grocery-ambitions-spell-trouble-for-big-food-brands
-1498469402.

Goel, Vindu, "Amazon, in Hunt for Lower Prices, Recruits Indian Merchants," *New York Times*, November 26, 2017, accessed February 25, 2018, https://www.nytimes.com/2017
/11/26/technology/amazon-india-merchants.html.

Hays, Kali, "Amazon Inks Violet Grey Deal: Sources," *WWD*, July 28, 2017, accessed February 25, 2018, http://wwd.com/business-news/financial/amazon-violet-grey
-second-quarter-luxury-beauty-10953327/.

Howland, Daphne, "Amazon Smashes Cyber Monday Record," *Retail Dive*, November 30, 2017, accessed February 24, 2018, https://www.retaildive.com/news
/amazon-smashes-cyber-monday-record/511975/.

Jarvey, Natalie, "Amazon's Hollywood Shopping Cart Secrets," *Hollywood Reporter*, July 15, 2015, accessed March 30, 2018, https://www.hollywoodreporter.com/features
/amazon-prime-day-hollywood-shopping-808533.

Kim, Eugene, "Amazon Quietly Launched an App Called Relay to Go after Truck Drivers," *CNBC*, November 16, 2017, accessed February 25, 2018, https://www.cnbc
.com/2017/11/16/amazon-quietly-launched-an-app-called-relay-to-go-after-truck
-drivers.html.

Kim, Tae, "Buy Amazon because Alexa Will Drive $10 Billion in Sales By 2020, RBC's Mahaney Predicts," *CNBC*, December 21, 2017, accessed February 24, 2018, https://
www.cnbc.com/2017/12/21/buy-amazon-because-alexa-will-drive-10-billion-in-sales
-rbc-capital.html.

Kim, W. Chan, Renee Mauborgne, and Oh Young Koo, "Amazon: Successes and Failures of Amazon's Growth Strategies: Causes and Consequences" (Case Study IN1397-PDF-ENG), *Harvard Business Review*, September 25, 2017, accessed February 24, 2018, https://hbr.org/product/successes-and-failures-of-amazons-growth
-strategies-causes-and-consequences/IN1397-PDF-ENG.

Kirby, Julia, and Thomas A. Stewart, "The Institutional Yes," *Harvard Business Review*, October 2007, accessed April 3, 2018, https://hbr.org/2007/10/the-institutional-yes.

Kittilaksanawong, Wiboon, and Auriela Karp, "Amazon Go: Venturing into Traditional Retail" (Case Study W17398-PDF-ENG), *Harvard Business Review*, June 28, 2017, accessed February 24, 2018, https://hbr.org/product/amazon-go-venturing-into
-traditional-retail/W17398-PDF-ENG.

Lashinsky, Adam, "Amazon's Jeff Bezos: The Ultimate Disrupter," *Fortune*, November 16, 2012, accessed March 30, 2018, http://fortune.com/2012/11/16/amazons-jeff-bezos-the
-ultimate-disrupter/.

Martinez, Michael, "Amazon: Everything You Wanted to Know about Its Algorithm and Innovation," *IEEE Internet Computing*, September 27, 2017, accessed February 24, 2018, https://www.computer.org/internet-computing/2017/09/27/amazon-all-the-research
-you-need-about-its-algorithm-and-innovation/.

Milnes, Hilary, "'Trapped': How Amazon Is Cornering Fashion Brands into Wholesale," *Glossy*, July 10, 2017, accessed February 26, 2018, http://www.glossy.co/the-amazon -effect/trapped-how-amazon-is-cornering-fashion-brands-into-wholesale.

Mims, Christopher, "The Limits of Amazon," *Wall Street Journal*, January 1, 2018, accessed April 3, 2018, https://www.wsj.com/articles/the-limits-of-amazon-1514808002.

Molla, Rani, and Jason Del Rey, "Amazon's Epic 20-Year Run as a Public Company, Explained in Five Charts," *Recode*, May 15, 2017, accessed February 24, 2018, https:// www.recode.net/2017/5/15/15610786/amazon-jeff-bezos-public-company-profit -revenue-explained-five-charts.

Reda, Susan, "21 Ways Amazon Changed the Face of Retail," *Stores Magazine*, September 2016, pp. 30–33.

———, "What's in Store for 2018?" *Stores Magazine*, December 4, 2017, accessed February 25, 2018, https://stores.org/2017/12/04/looking-forward/.

Rigby, Darrell K., "The Amazon–Whole Foods Deal Means Every Other Retailer's Three-Year Plan Is Obsolete," *Harvard Business Review*, June 21, 2017, accessed February 24, 2018, https://hbr.org/2017/06/the-amazon-whole-foods-deal-means-every -other-retailers-three-year-plan-is-obsolete.

Robischon, Noah, "Why Amazon Is the World's Most Innovative Company of 2017," *Fast Company*, February 13, 2017, accessed February 24, 2018, https://www.fastcompany.com /3067455/why-amazon-is-the-worlds-most-innovative-company-of-2017.

Ruff, Corinne, "Are Calvin Klein's Amazon Pop-Ups Dissing Department Stores?" *Retail Dive*, November 29, 2017, accessed February 25, 2018, https://www.retaildive .com/news/are-calvin-kleins-amazon-pop-ups-dissing-department-stores/511700/.

Schmid, Helen, "Competitive Strategy: Should You Compete with Amazon or Sell on Amazon?" *Harvard Business Review*, May 23, 2016, accessed February 24, 2018, https:// hbr.org/2016/05/should-you-compete-with-amazon-or-sell-on-amazon.

Scott, Dylan, "What to Make of Amazon and Warren Buffett's Mystery Health Care Project," *Vox*, January 31, 2018, accessed February 24, 2018, https://www.vox.com /technology/2018/1/31/16950500/amazon-health-care-jp-morgan-chase-warren-buffett.

Siegel, Richie, "Op-Ed: Will the Digitally Native Brand Building Playbook Produce Results?," *The Business of Fashion*, November 29, 2017, accessed April 3, 2018, https://www.businessoffashion.com/articles/opinion/op-ed-will-the-digital-native-brand -building-playbook-produce-results.

Skrovan, Sandy, "Report: Amazon and Whole Foods to Thrive by Nabbing Each Other's Customers," *Retail Dive*, September 15, 2017, accessed February 24, 2018, http://www .retaildive.com/news/report-amazon-and-whole-foods-to-thrive-by-nabbing-each -others-customers/505050/.

Spector, Robert, "The Rise and Fall of Toys 'R' Us," *The Robin Report*, October 18, 2017, accessed February 25, 2018, http://www.therobinreport.com/the-rise-and-fall-of-toys -r-us/.

Stevens, Laura, "Amazon Delays Opening of Cashierless Store to Work Out Kinks," *Wall Street Journal,* March 27, 2017, accessed February 25, 2018, https://www.wsj.com/articles/amazon-delays-convenience-store-opening-to-work-out-kinks-1490616133.

Stevens, Laura, and Sara Germano, "Nike Thought It Didn't Need Amazon—Then the Ground Shifted," *Wall Street Journal,* June 28, 2017, accessed February 25, 2018, https://www.wsj.com/articles/how-nike-resisted-amazons-dominance-for-years-and-finally-capitulated-1498662435.

Thompson, Derek, "Why Amazon Bought Whole Foods," *The Atlantic,* June 16, 2017, accessed February 24, 2018, https://www.theatlantic.com/business/archive/2017/06/why-amazon-bought-whole-foods/530652/.

Thomson, James, "Strategies to Be Successful Selling on Amazon in 2018," *International Business Times,* November 21, 2017, accessed February 24, 2018, http://www.ibtimes.com/5-strategies-be-successful-selling-amazon-2018-2617932.

US Securities and Exchange Commission, "2015 Letter to Shareholders," April 24, 2015, accessed April 3, 2018, https://www.sec.gov/Archives/edgar/data/1018724/000119312516530910/d168744dex991.htm.

Wells, John R., Gale Danskin, and Gabriel Ellsworth, "Amazon.com, 2016," Harvard Business School Case 9-716-402, May 16, 2016, accessed February 26, 2018, https://www.scribd.com/document/370797374/Amazon.

Chapter 3

Bose, Nandita, "Exclusive: Aldi Raises Stakes in U.S. Price War with Wal-Mart," *Reuters,* May 11, 2017, accessed February 26, 2018, http://www.reuters.com/article/us-aldi-walmart-pricing-exclusive/exclusive-aldi-raises-stakes-in-u-s-price-war-with-wal-mart-idUSKBN1870EN.

Chen, Oliver, "Target: Expect More, Pay Less . . . & Go from Crunches to Brunches," Cowen Report, August 16, 2017.

Cheng, Andria, "Dollar Stores' Growth Opportunities—and Challenges," *eMarketerRetail,* June 1, 2017, accessed February 24, 2018, https://retail.emarketer.com/article/dollar-stores-growth-opportunitiesand-challenges/59308c35ebd4000b2ceae02d.

Clark, Evan, and Sharon Edelson, "Buying the Future: Amazon, Walmart Cut Deals to Compete," *WWD,* June 19, 2017, accessed February 24, 2018, http://wwd.com/business-news/financial/amazon-wal-mart-jet-whole-foods-marc-lore-jeff-bezos-retail-ecommerce-acquisition-10917720/.

Clifford, Stephanie, "Where Wal-Mart Failed, Aldi Succeeds," *New York Times,* March 29, 2011, accessed February 24, 2018, http://www.nytimes.com/2011/03/30/business/30aldi.html.

Del Ray, Jason, "Walmart Has Acquired the Logistics Startup Parcel to Help Launch Same-Day Delivery in New York City," *Recode,* October 3, 2017, accessed February 24, 2018, https://www.recode.net/2017/10/3/16405158/walmart-parcel-acquisition-logistics-same-day-delivery-startup.

Edelson, Sharon, "Wal-Mart's New Focus: Technology Is Priority, Not Super Centers," *WWD*, October 10, 2017, accessed February 24, 2018, http://wwd.com /business-news/retail/wal-marts-2017-analyst-meeting-technology-is-buzzword -11024483/.

The Hartman Group, "ALDI Is a Growing Menace to America's Grocery Retailers," *Forbes*, April 14, 2015, accessed February 24, 2018, https://www.forbes.com/sites/thehartmangroup /2015/04/14/aldi-is-a-growing-menace-to-americas-grocery-retailers/#42d8a711f077.

Hirsch, Lauren, "Jet Launches Its Own Private Label Brand, Uniquely J," *CNBC*, October 20, 2017, accessed February 24, 2018, https://www.cnbc.com/2017/10/20/jet -launches-private-label-brand-uniquely-j.html.

Howland, Daphne, "Jet Takes on Amazon, Target with New Private Brand 'Uniquely J'," *Retail Dive*, October 24, 2017, accessed March 26, 2018, https://www.retaildive.com /news/jet-takes-on-amazon-target-with-new-private-brand-uniquely-j/507983/.

———, "Why Walmart Is Betting Big on E-Commerce Acquisitions," *Retail Dive*, May 31, 2017, accessed February 24, 2018, https://www.retaildive.com/news/why-wal -mart-is-betting-big-on-e-commerce-acquisitions/443177/.

———, "Walmart Reportedly Testing Amazon Go-Like Store, Personal Shopping Service," *Retail Dive*, December 21, 2017, accessed February 24, 2018, https://www .retaildive.com/news/walmart-reportedly-testing-amazon-go-like-store-personal -shopping-service/513610/.

Irwin, Neil, "The Amazon-Walmart Showdown that Explains the Modern Economy," *New York Times*, June 16, 2017, accessed February 24, 2018, https://www.nytimes.com /2017/06/16/upshot/the-amazon-walmart-showdown-that-explains-the-modern -economy.html.

Kelleher, Kevin, "How Walmart Uses AI to Serve 140 Million Customers a Week," *Venture Beat*, July 11, 2017, accessed February 24, 2018, https://venturebeat.com/2017 /07/11/how-walmart-uses-ai-to-serve-140-million-customers-a-week/.

Mattern, Jessica Leigh, "Here's the Real Reason Everyone Loves Aldi So Much," *Country Living*, October 6, 2017, accessed February 24, 2018, http://www.countryliving.com /food-drinks/news/a45149/how-aldi-stores-work/.

Mondloch, Emily, "It's a New Day for Dollar Stores," Baber Martin Agency, September 15, 2017, accessed February 24, 2018, https://www.barbermartin.com/dollar -stores-retail-expansion/.

O'Shea, Don, "How Walmart Is Using Tech This Holiday Season," *Retail Dive*, November 26, 2017, accessed February 24, 2018, https://www.retaildive.com/news/how -walmart-is-using-tech-this-holiday-season/511607/.

Ruff, Corinne, "Walmart's Store No. 8 Showcases the Future of VR," *Retail Dive*, October 19, 2017, accessed February 24, 2018, https://www.retaildive.com/news /walmarts-store-no-8-showcases-the-future-of-vr/507639/.

Soper, Taylor, "How STRIVR Expanded Its VR Sport Training Platform to Walmart Associates and NFL Referees," *GeekWire*, August 18, 2017, accessed February 24, 2018,

https://www.geekwire.com/2017/strivr-expanded-vr-sports-training-platform-walmart
-associates-nfl-referees/.

Thomas, Lauren, and Courtney Reagan, "Take that Alexa! Walmart Partners with
Google to Offer Voice Shopping," *CNBC*, August 23, 2017, accessed February 24, 2018,
https://www.cnbc.com/2017/08/22/wal-mart-partners-with-google-to-offer-voice
-shopping-via-google-home.html.

"Walmart: Thinking Outside the Box," *The Economist*, June 4, 2016, accessed
February 24, 2018, https://www.economist.com/news/business/21699961-american
-shoppers-move-online-walmart-fights-defend-its-dominance-thinking-outside.

Chapter 4

Chu, Melissa, "The Unconventional Strategy Zara Used to Dominate an Industry (and
What We Can Do to Mirror Its Success)," *The Mission*, September 12, 2017, accessed
February 25, 2018, https://medium.com/the-mission/the-unconventional-strategy-zara
-used-to-dominate-an-industry-and-what-we-can-do-to-mirror-its-4078698c08e0.

Dunn, Andy, "The Book of DNVB: The Rise of Digitally Native Vertical Brands,"
Medium, May 9, 2016, accessed February 25, 2018, https://medium.com/@dunn
/digitally-native-vertical-brands-b26a26f2cf83.

Howland, Daphne, "Nordstrom Opening Merchandise-Free Concept," *Retail Dive*,
September 11, 2017, accessed February 25, 2018, http://www.retaildive.com/news
/nordstrom-opening-merchandise-free-concept/504655/.

Kowsmann, Patricia, "Zara's Strategy: Bigger Stores, Online Push," *MarketWatch*,
March 16, 2017, accessed February 25, 2018, https://www.marketwatch.com/story/zaras
-strategy-bigger-stores-online-push-2017-03-16.

Lutz, Ashley, "This Clothing Company Whose CEO Is Richer than Warren Buffett Is
Blowing the Competition Out of the Water," *Business Insider*, June 13, 2015, accessed
February 25, 2018, http://www.businessinsider.com/zaras-retail-strategy-is-winning
-2015-6.

Mang, Lauren, "The Un-Store: High-End Stores That Don't Actually Sell Anything Are
the Future of Retail," *Quartz*, November 24, 2017, accessed February 25, 2018, https://qz
.com/1135230/high-end-stores-that-dont-actually-sell-anything-are-the-future-of
-retail/.

Neumann, Jeannette, "How Zara Is Defying a Broad Retail Slump," *Wall Street Journal*,
June 14, 2017, accessed February 25, 2018, https://www.wsj.com/articles/how-zara-is
-defying-a-broad-retail-slump-1497467742.

"Our Story," Trader Joe's homepage, accessed February 25, 2018, https://www.traderjoes
.com/our-story.

Roll, Martin, "The Secret of Zara's Success: A Culture of Customer Co-Creation,"
Martin Roll Business & Brand Leadership, December 2016, accessed February 25, 2018,
https://martinroll.com/resources/articles/strategy/the-secret-of-zaras-success-a-culture
-of-customer-co-creation/.

Siegel, Richie, "From a Digitally-Native Gold Rush to an Impending Bloodbath," *Loose Threads*, October 20, 2017, accessed February 26, 2018, https://loosethreads.com /espresso/2017/10/19/digitally-native-gold-rush-impending-bloodbath/.

————, "Op-Ed: Will the Digitally Native Brand Building Playbook Produce Results?" *The Business of Fashion*, November 29, 2017, accessed February 25, 2018, https://www .businessoffashion.com/articles/opinion/op-ed-will-the-digital-native-brand-building -playbook-produce-results.

Taylor, Kate, "Whole Foods Is Cutting Prices—and It's Hitting Trader Joe's Hard," *Business Insider*, October 3, 2017, accessed February 25, 2018, http://www .businessinsider.com/amazon-buys-whole-foods-hurts-trader-joes-target-2017-10.

"The Top 25 Digitally Native Vertical Brands 2017" (white paper), *Pixlee*, 2017, accessed February 25, 2018, https://www.pixlee.com/download/the-top-digitally-native-brands -report-for-2017.

Varma, Ankita, "Zara's Secret to Success Lies in Big Data and an Agile Supply Chain," *Straits Times*, May 25, 2017, accessed February 25, 2018, http://www.straitstimes.com /lifestyle/fashion/zaras-secret-to-success-lies-in-big-data-and-an-agile-supply -chain.

Welch, Liz, "How Casper Became a $100 Million Company in Less Than Two Years," *Inc.*, February 25, 2016, accessed February 25, 2018, https://www.inc.com/magazine /201603/liz-welch/casper-changing-mattress-industry.html.

Wilson, Marianne, "Hot Online Mattress Start-Up Delves into Brick-and-Mortar," *Chain Store Age*, November 1, 2017, accessed February 25, 2018, https://www .chainstoreage.com/store-spaces/hot-online-mattress-start-delves-brick-mortar/.

Wohletz, Jenn, "Top Five Reasons Why People Love Trader Joe's So F*@%ing Much," *Westword*, February 17, 2012, accessed February 25, 2018, http://www.westword.com /restaurants/top-five-reasons-why-people-love-trader-joes-so-f-ing-much-5773473.

Chapter 5

Alvarez, Edgar, "The World of High Fashion Finally Has Its Answer to Amazon," *Engadget*, July 13, 2017, accessed February 25, 2018, https://www.engadget.com/2017 /07/13/lvmh-24-sevres-interview/.

Berezhna, Victoria, "The Art of the Markdown," *The Business of Fashion*, December 15, 2017, accessed February 25, 2018, https://www.businessoffashion.com/articles /intelligence/the-art-of-the-markdown.

Berthon, Pierre, Leyland F. Pitt, Michael Parent, and Jean-Paul Berthon, "Aesthetics and Ephemerality: Observing and Preserving the Luxury Brand," *California Management Review*, November 1, 2009, accessed February 25, 2018, http://cmr.berkeley.edu/search /articleDetail.aspx?article=5538.

Binkley, Christina, "At Luxury Stores, It Isn't Shopping, It's an Experience," *Wall Street Journal*, April 16, 2017, accessed February 25, 2018, https://www.wsj.com/articles/at -luxury-stores-it-isnt-shopping-its-an-experience-1492394460.

Clark, Evan, "Louis Vuitton x Supreme: A 100M Euro Boost for Skate Brand's Luxe Cred," *WWD*, October 13, 2017, accessed February 25, 2018, http://wwd.com/business -news/financial/louis-vuitton-supreme-carlyle-100m-skate-brand-luxury-11026636/.

Danziger, Pamela N., "Luxury Brands Innovation Is No Luxury, but a Necessity," *Forbes*, August 8, 2017, accessed February 25, 2018, https://www.forbes.com/sites/pamdanziger /2017/08/08/luxury-brands-innovation-is-no-luxury-but-a-necessity/2/#4876cf9c4be5.

Doupnik, Elizabeth, "2018 Retail Predictions: AI, Experiences, Pricing Transparency to Increase," *WWD*, December 4, 2017, accessed February 25, 2018, http://wwd.com /business-news/retail/edited-2018-retail-forecast-11062611/.

"Global Personal Luxury Goods Market Returns to Health Growth, Reaching a Fresh High of 262 Billion Euros in 2017," *Bain & Company*, October 25, 2017, accessed February 25, 2018, http://www.bain.com/about/press/press-releases/press-release-2017 -global-fall-luxury-market-study.aspx.

Halzack, Sarah, "American Luxury Brands Remember to Be Luxurious," *Bloomberg Gadfly*, November 6, 2017, accessed February 25, 2018, https://www.bloomberg.com /gadfly/articles/2017-11-06/michael-kors-earnings-luxury-wins-by-being-luxurious.

Han, Young Jee, Joseph C. Nunes, and Xavier Drèze, "Signaling Status with Luxury Goods: The Role of Brand Prominence," *Journal of Marketing*, July 2010, accessed February 25, 2018, http://journals.ama.org/doi/abs/10.1509/jmkg.74.4.15?code=amma-site.

Howland, Daphne, "Coach Rebrands as 'Tapestry,'" *Retail Dive*, October 12, 2017, accessed February 25, 2018, http://www.retaildive.com/news/coach-rebrands-as -tapestry/507146/.

Kapferer, J. N., *Kapferer on Luxury: How Luxury Brands Can Grow Yet Remain Rare* (Philadelphia: Kogan Page Publishers, 2015)

Milnes, Hilary, "How China's Luxury E-Commerce Market Will Evolve in 2018," *Glossy*, December 15, 2017, accessed February 26, 2018, http://www.glossy.co/year-in-review /how-chinas-luxury-e-commerce-market-will-evolve-in-2018.

Paton, Elizabeth, "Imagining the Retail Store of the Future," *New York Times*, April 12, 2017, accessed February 26, 2018, https://www.nytimes.com/2017/04/12/fashion/store -of-the-future.html.

———, "Europe's Luxury Retailers May be Returning to Form," *New York Times*, July 28, 2017, accessed February 25, 2018, https://www.nytimes.com/2017/07/28/business /luxury-brands-europe-gucci-lvmh.html.

———, "LVMH and the Next Big Digital Shopping Experience," *New York Times*, May 10, 2017, accessed February 25, 2018, https://www.nytimes.com/2017/05/10 /fashion/lvmh-ian-rogers-24-sevres-takes-on-amazon.html.

Puleo, Melissa, "The Secret Rise of Digital Strategy for Luxury Brands," *Decoded: Contemporary Commerce*, October 24, 2017, accessed February 25, 2018, https://www .salsify.com/blog/digital-strategy-for-luxury-brands.

Salpini, Cara, "Study: Gen Z More Likely Than Millennials to Buy Luxury Brands," *Retail Dive*, July 7, 2017, accessed February 25, 2018, https://www.retaildive.com/news /study-gen-z-more-likely-than-millennials-to-buy-luxury-brands/446623/.

Sherman, Lauren, "Marc Jacobs to Close London Store and Other European Outposts," *The Business of Fashion*, January 5, 2018, accessed February 25, 2018, https://www.businessoffashion.com/articles/news-analysis/marc-jacobs-to-close-london-store-and-other-european-outposts.

Smith, Katie, "The Retail Landscape in 2018," *Edited*, December 21, 2017, accessed February 26, 2018, https://edited.com/blog/2017/12/retail-trends-of-2018/.

Thomas, Lauren, "Michael Kors Hikes 2018 Outlook, Sending Shares of the Handbag Maker Higher," *CNBC*, November 6, 2017, accessed February 25, 2018, https://www.cnbc.com/2017/11/06/michael-kors-hikes-2018-outlook-sending-luxury-retailers-shares-up.html.

Wahba, Phil, "Coach Thinks Outside the Bag," *Fortune*, May 24, 2017, accessed February 25, 2018, http://fortune.com/2017/05/24/coach-victor-luis-stuart-vevers/.

Chapter 6

Baird-Remba, Rebecca, "Are Off-Price Retailers Truly Amazon-Proof?" *Commercial Observer*, December 7, 2017, accessed February 26, 2018, https://commercialobserver.com/2017/12/are-off-price-retailers-truly-amazon-proof/.

Bhattarai, Abha, "Will Millennials Kill Costco?" *Washington Post*, January 19, 2018, accessed February 25, 2018, https://www.washingtonpost.com/business/economy/will-millennials-kill-costco/2018/01/19/d0de5dec-fb9e-11e7-a46b-a3614530bd87_story.html?utm_term=.23ee0ccd9277.

Bloomberg, "The TJ Maxx Strategy: How One Huge American Retailer Ignored the Internet and Won," *The Business of Fashion*, December 21, 2016, accessed February 25, 2018, https://www.businessoffashion.com/articles/news-analysis/how-one-huge-american-retailer-ignored-the-internet-and-won.

Cuozzo, Steve, "The Complex Economics of NYC's Food Hall Glut," *New York Post*, January 18, 2018, accessed February 25, 2018, https://nypost.com/2018/01/18/the-complex-economics-of-nycs-food-hall-glut/.

Estes, Diane Lincoln, "In the Age of Amazon, an Entrepreneur Explains What Will Make Us Want to Go to the Store," *PBS NewsHour*, August 24, 2017, accessed February 25, 2018, https://www.pbs.org/newshour/economy/age-amazon-entrepreneur-explains-will-make-us-want-go-store.

Filloon, Whitney, "Eataly Eyes IPO in 2018," *Eater*, December 11, 2017, accessed February 25, 2018, https://www.eater.com/2017/12/11/16762716/eataly-ipo-2018.

———, "How Eataly Became an Italian Food Superpower," *Eater*, October 30, 2017, accessed February 25, 2018, https://www.eater.com/2016/8/12/12442512/eataly-history-store-locations.

Gibson, Ellen, "Hidden Treasures Drive Impulse Buys: Surprises in Stores Lure Customers to Spend More," *Boston.com*, July 6, 2011, accessed February 25, 2018, http://archive.boston.com/business/articles/2011/07/06/hidden_treasures_drive_impulse_buys/.

Howland, Daphne, "Costco 'Destroys' November with Massive Sales Surge," *Retail Dive*, November 30, 2017, accessed February 25, 2018, https://www.retaildive.com/news/costco-destroys-november-with-massive-sales-surge/511990/.

———, "Costco Sales Soar 14.3% in December," *Retail Dive*, January 5, 2018, accessed February 25, 2018, https://www.retaildive.com/news/costco-sales-soar-143-in -december/514141/.

Kestenbaum, Richard, "Soaring Off-Price Retail Chains May Be Set for a Fall," *Forbes*, November 15, 2017, accessed February 25, 2018, https://www.forbes.com/sites /richardkestenbaum/2017/11/15/the-off-price-business-is-more-troubled-than-it-looks /#26ffa9ed1554.

Kowitt, Beth, "Is T.J. Maxx the Best Retail Store in the Land?" *Fortune*, July 24, 2014, accessed February 25, 2018, http://fortune.com/2014/07/24/t-j-maxx-the-best-retail-store/.

Mahoney, Sarah, "Buoyed by Instacart, Costco Seems Amazon-Proof," *Marketing Daily*, December 18, 2017, accessed February 25, 2018, https://www.mediapost.com /publications/article/311803/buoyed-by-instacart-costco-seems-amazon-proof.html.

Meyrowitz, Carol, "How I Did It: The CEO of TJX on How to Train," *Harvard Business Review*, May 2014, Reprint R1405A.

Milnes, Hilary, "How Tech in Rebecca Minkoff's Fitting Rooms Tripled Expected Clothing Sales," *Digiday*, September 25, 2015, accessed February 25, 2018, https:// digiday.com/marketing/rebecca-minkoff-digital-store/.

———, "Rebecca Minkoff Uses VR for Planning Stores," *Glossy*, November 30, 2017, accessed February 25, 2018, http://www.glossy.co/store-of-the-future/rebecca-minkoff -uses-vr-for-planning-stores.

Nassauer, Sarah, "How Kirkland Signature Became One of Costco's Biggest Success Stories," *Wall Street Journal*, September 10, 2017, accessed February 25, 2018, https:// www.wsj.com/articles/how-kirkland-signature-became-one-of-costcos-biggest-success -stories-1505041202.

O'Connor, Clare, "No Trick, Just Treat: Halloween Pop-Ups Now Account for Half Spencer Gifts' Annual Sales," *Forbes*, October 11, 2013, accessed February 25, 2018, https://www.forbes.com/sites/clareoconnor/2013/10/11/no-trick-just-treat-halloween -pop-ups-now-account-for-half-spencer-gifts-annual-sales/#48baf6ff317a.

Pasquarelli, Adrianne, "How TJX Crafted a Winning Marketing Playbook," *Adage*, May 23, 2016, accessed February 25, 2018, http://adage.com/article/cmo-strategy/award -find-retailer-winning/304117/.

Salpini, Cara, "30 Minutes with Sephora's Head of Marketing," *Retail Dive*, November 29, 2017, accessed February 25, 2018, https://www.retaildive.com/news/30 -minutes-with-sephoras-head-of-marketing/510300/.

———, "Will Amazon Give Beauty a Makeover?" *Retail Dive*, January 11, 2018, accessed February 25, 2018, https://www.retaildive.com/news/will-amazon-give-beauty -a-makeover/514544/.

Thomas, Lauren, "Pop-Up Shop Pioneer Spirit Halloween Is Hitting the Mall as More Retailers Vacate," *CNBC*, October 5, 2017, accessed February 25, 2018, https://www .cnbc.com/2017/10/05/halloween-pop-up-shops-expand-us-footprint-other-retailers -vacate.html.

Twilley, Nicola, and Cynthia Graber, "A Glimpse into the World's First Italian-Food Theme Park," *The Atlantic*, October 23, 2017, accessed February 26, 2018, https://www.theatlantic.com/science/archive/2017/10/eataly-future-of-supermarkets/543678/.

Wells, Jeff, "Costco's Strong Q1 Earnings Prove It's Still Amazon-Proof," *Retail Dive*, December 15, 2017, accessed February 25, 2018, https://www.retaildive.com/news/costcos-strong-q1-earnings-prove-its-still-amazon-proof/513185/.

Yohn, Denise Lee, "Big-Box Retailers Have Two Options If They Want to Survive," *Harvard Business Review*, June 22, 2016, accessed February 26, 2018, https://hbr.org/2016/06/big-box-retailers-have-two-options-if-they-want-to-survive.

Conclusion

Fernandez, Chantal, "J.Crew, Gap, Abercrombie & Fitch: The Trouble with America's Most Beloved Mall Brands," *The Business of Fashion*, January 9, 2017, accessed February 25, 2018, https://www.businessoffashion.com/articles/intelligence/gap-j-crew-abercrombie-trouble-americas-mall-brands.

Ruff, Corinne, "7 Retail Execs Envision the Future of Stores," *Retail Dive*, February 13, 2018, accessed February 25, 2018, https://www.retaildive.com/news/7-retail-execs-envision-the-future-of-stores/516795/.

Wahba, Phil, "Gap Inc. Is Closing 200 Stores but Opening 270 New Ones," *Fortune*, September 6, 2017, accessed February 25, 2018, http://fortune.com/2017/09/06/gap-inc-banana-republic-old-navy/.

———, "Macy's Sales Decline for the 10th Straight Quarter," *Fortune*, August 10, 2017, accessed February 25, 2018, http://fortune.com/2017/08/10/macys-sales-decline-2/.

Appendix

Ruff, Corinne, "7 Retail Execs Envision the Future of Stores," *Retail Dive*, February 13, 2018, accessed February 24, 2018, https://www.retaildive.com/news/7-retail-execs-envision-the-future-of-stores/516795/.

Index

Note: Page numbers in italics refer to figures or tables.

About the Author

Barbara E. Kahn is Patty and Jay H. Baker Professor of Marketing at The Wharton School at the University of Pennsylvania. She served two terms as the director of the Jay H. Baker Retailing Center. Prior to rejoining Wharton in 2011, Barbara served as the dean and Schein Professor of Marketing at the School of Business Administration, University of Miami (from 2007 to 2011). Before becoming dean at UM, she spent 17 years at Wharton as Silberberg Professor of Marketing. She was also vice dean of the Wharton undergraduate program.

Barbara is an internationally recognized scholar on retailing, variety seeking, brand loyalty, product assortment and design, and consumer and patient decision-making. She has published more than 75 articles in leading academic journals. In addition to *The Shopping Revolution,* she is the author of *Global Brand Power: Leveraging Branding for Long-Term Growth* and coauthor of *Grocery Revolution: The New Focus on the Consumer.*

Barbara has been elected president of the Association for Consumer Research, elected president of the Journal of Consumer Research (JCR) Policy Board, and selected as a Marketing Science Institute trustee. She was also an associate editor at *JCR, Journal of Marketing,* and *Marketing Science.* She has recently been elected as a fellow for both the Association of Consumer Research and the Society of Consumer Psychology.

Barbara received her PhD, MBA, and MPhil from Columbia University, and her BA from the University of Rochester.

About Wharton Digital Press

Wharton Digital Press was established to inspire bold, insightful thinking within the global business community. In the tradition of The Wharton School of the University of Pennsylvania and its online business journal, Knowledge@Wharton, Wharton Digital Press uses innovative digital technologies to help managers meet the challenges of today and tomorrow.

As an entrepreneurial publisher, Wharton Digital Press delivers relevant, accessible, conceptually sound and empirically based business knowledge to readers wherever and whenever they need it. Its format ranges from ebooks to print books available through print-on-demand technology. Directed to a general business audience, the Press's areas of interest include management and strategy, innovation and entrepreneurship, finance and investment, leadership, marketing, operations, human resources, social responsibility and business–government relations.

http://wdp.wharton.upenn.edu/

Wharton
UNIVERSITY *of* PENNSYLVANIA

About The Wharton School

Founded in 1881 as the first collegiate business school, The Wharton School of the University of Pennsylvania is recognized globally for intellectual leadership and ongoing innovation across every major discipline of business education. With a broad global community and one of the most published business school faculties, Wharton creates economic and social value around the world. The School has 5,000 undergraduate, MBA, executive MBA, and doctoral students; more than 9,000 participants in executive education programs annually; and a powerful alumni network of 96,000 graduates.

http://wdp.wharton.upenn.edu/